D0070115

THE ALAMO
IN AMERICAN HISTORY

IN AMERICAN HISTORY

THE ALAMO
IN AMERICAN HISTORY

Roy Sorrels

Enslow Publishers, Inc.

44 Fadem Road	PO Box 38
Box 699	Aldershot
Springfield, NJ 07081	Hants GU12 6BP
USA	UK

Library of Congress Cataloging-in-Publication Data

Sorrels, Roy.
    The Alamo in American history / Roy Sorrels.
        p. cm. — (In American history)
        Includes bibliographical references (p.) and index.
        Summary: Gives an in-depth account of the battle at the Alamo and
    discusses the conflicts which led up to it.
        ISBN 0-89490-770-0
        1. Alamo (San Antonio, Tex.)—Siege, 1836—Juvenile literature.
        2. Alamo (San Antonio, Tex.)—Siege, 1836—Causes—Juvenile literature.
        3. Texas—History—Revolution, 1835-1836—Juvenile literature. [1.
    Alamo (San Antonio, Tex.)—Siege, 1836. 2. Texas—History—Revolution,
    1835-1836.] I. Title. II. Series.
    F390.S72 1996
    976.4'351—dc20   96-5782
                                                               CIP
                                                                AC
Printed in the United States of America

10 9 8 7 6 5 4 3 2 1

Illustration Credits: Archives Division, Texas State Library, pp. 61, 79,
103; © 1996 Carolyn J. Yaschur, pp. 10, 15, 70, 115; Courtesy of the
Texas State Library, *The Dictionary of American Portraits*, published by
Dover Publications, Inc., in 1967, pp. 22, 36; Engraved by Thomas B.
Welch from a painting by S.S. Osgood, *The Dictionary of American Portraits*,
published by Dover Publications, Inc., in 1967, p. 47; Enslow Publishers,
Inc., pp. 67, 87, 108; *The Dictionary of American Portraits*, published by
Dover Publications, Inc., in 1967, pp. 11, 25, 44; Painting by Edward
Schnabel. Courtesy of Gregory's Old Master Gallery, *The Dictionary of
American Portraits*, published by Dover Publications, Inc., in 1967, p. 33;
Painting by Paul L'Ouvrier. Courtesy New-York Historical Society, *The
Dictionary of American Portraits*, published by Dover Publications, Inc., in
1967, p. 21; Photograph by Mathew Brady, *The Dictionary of American
Portraits*, published by Dover Publications, Inc., in 1967, p. 113; Robert L.
Pigeon III, Combined Books, pp. 54, 72; Texas Department of
Transportation, p. 52; Library of Congress, pp. 13, 41, 83, 97; © Corel
Corporation, 1994, p. 18.

Cover Illustration: Engraved by Thomas B. Welch from a painting by
S.S. Osgood, *The Dictionary of American Portraits*, published by Dover
Publications, Inc., in 1967; Enslow Publishers, Inc.; Archives Division,
Texas State Library; © 1996 Carolyn J. Yaschur.

★ CONTENTS ★

"REMEMBER THE ALAMO"

General Antonio López de Santa Anna and his army of four thousand Mexican solders marched north on that frosty winter of 1836 toward San Antonio. Inside the Alamo, a former Spanish mission complex turned into a fortress, the Texas defenders gathered ready to fight. Few of them had realized how quickly Santa Anna could bring a large army over such a great distance. Now they were to feel the full extent of his determination and anger.

Winning the battle against Mexican General Martin Perfect de Cos and taking San Antonio and the Alamo in December 1835 had been simple. The Texans had won easily, driving the Mexican general and his army back into Mexico in disgrace. Then winter had come and many thought that there would be no more fighting for the time being. So many of the Texas troops simply wandered off or headed home to their families.

The defenders inside the Alamo were not preparing as well or as carefully as they could have been. This was partly due to inexperience and lack of organization, but also because they generally held the Mexican Army in contempt.

While Santa Anna moved north, no one in Texas seemed to be paying much attention. Even Sam Houston, by now in charge of the Texas army, went off to negotiate a treaty with the Texas Cherokees to keep them neutral in the conflict.

Jim Bowie and his company of twenty to thirty men arrived at the Alamo in late January. They had to decide whether or not to blow it up so that it would not fall into Mexico's hands. Lieutenant Colonel James C. Neill, who was in charge, did not paint a very encouraging picture for Bowie. Only about 115 soldiers were still at the Alamo, and some of them were still recovering from the battle against General Cos. Supplies—and more importantly, ammunition—were low.

Even though Bowie had permission to destroy the Alamo, both he and Neill elected not to do so. Bowie wrote to the Texas government: "The salvation of Texas depends in great measure in keeping Bejar [San Antonio] out of the hands of the enemy. . . . Colonel Neill and myself have come to the solemn resolution that we will rather die in these ditches than give up this post to the enemy."[1]

The next day, Lieutenant Colonel William B. Travis and thirty cavalrymen arrived at the Alamo. Texas Governor Henry Smith had given Travis orders to help reinforce the Alamo. In the battle that would follow, all of the Texan defenders would be killed. "Remember the Alamo" would become the battle cry for Texas independence.

When the first American settlers arrived, the vast land known as Texas was almost empty. In all that vastness there were no major cities as we know them today. There were a few Spanish colonial settlements and

★ 2 ★

A VAST LAND

a sparse scattering of missions—small religious settlements founded by Catholic priests to try to convert the Native Americans to Christianity.

Comanches, Lipan Apaches, and other tribes wandered freely, as they had for hundreds of years. Few roads crossed the enormous emptiness, only rough paths that the buffalo followed.

Although the huge space was almost empty, it was at the same time filled with danger. Across the broad plains, danger lurked in possible attacks from the Comanches and Apaches. The very emptiness of the land was dangerous in itself—there were few doctors to call on if someone got sick or broke a bone. A simple cut could become infected and cause death.

Yet the settlers came as early as 1810. They came in small family groups and as solo frontiersmen, hardy and sturdy. They sought freedom from too much government and not enough opportunity. The hunger for land of their own was one of the qualities that defined Americans of the time.

Spanish Influences

This huge expanse into which they moved was then part of the colony of New Spain.

In 1519, Hernando Cortés, a Spanish soldier and adventurer, had been sent across the sea by the Spanish rulers in search of gold and silver. The Spanish economy of the time, and the European economy as well, was hampered by the lack of silver and gold to make into coins. An economy that barters its product

Although seemingly empty to the first white settlers, Texas was inhabited by Native Americans and plenty of wildlife. The vast land held many dangers for the settlers.

for gold can only develop so far without more and more gold, so the Europeans needed more currency.

Cortés, driven by this hunger for gold and silver, conquered the land that had been ruled by the Aztecs throughout Mexico. His troops brought with them their fine Spanish horses. Indeed, it was partly because the Spaniards were mounted and the Aztecs were not that the Europeans were able to march west from Veracruz and overpower the mighty Montezuma, king of the Aztec Empire.

The land of the Aztecs then became a colony of Spain. Spanish missionaries, often at the point of a sword, set out to convert the Native Americans to

Hernando Cortés, an adventurer from Spain, conquered the Aztecs in the sixteenth century. This led to three hundred years of Spanish control of Mexico.

Christianity. Thousands of Aztecs and members of other tribes died—many from diseases that the Spaniards brought with them and many more from working under slave-labor conditions to mine silver and gold.

The Comanches

Over the next couple of hundred years, the Comanches, as well as the Apaches and some other Plains tribes, obtained horses descended from the noble Spanish steeds. The Comanches soon became expert riders. Children, women, and men all rode; and they rode very well. Horses allowed them to follow the gigantic buffalo herds and hunt them more easily. For the Comanches, living was relatively easy because the buffalo provided them with an abundant supply of food. The buffalo also provided hides for warm clothing and buffalo chips—dried manure—for fuel.

The Comanches never planted a seed and never settled down in villages. Their horses made it possible to hunt the buffalo and other game—including pronghorn antelope, deer, rabbits, elk, and turkeys—and to roam far and wide.

They became one of the most powerful and dangerous mounted attack forces in history. Armed with a long lance and a shield of buffalo hide tough enough to deflect a musket ball, the Comanche brave was also able to let loose a shower of arrows while riding at a full gallop. With a thong that wrapped around the

The Comanches were wanderers who lived off of the land. Warriors on horseback hunted the plentiful game using bow and arrows skillfully.

horse's body, a warrior could hang over one side for protection while thundering past an enemy.[1]

The Comanches were free nomads in an enormous sea of grass—with breakfast, lunch, and dinner just an arrow-shot away. They warred with the Apaches from time to time, but no other tribe could do more than get out of their way.

When a few settlers started to come to Texas in the 1700s, the Apaches were the primary tribe in colonial Texas. The Comanches arrived from the Plains around 1750, and soon they were so powerful and so much in control that the land was popularly referred to as "Comancheria," literally "land of the Comanche."

The Native Americans who followed the vast herds of buffalo could meet most of their needs with a few hours of hunting every few days. Imagine how they must have viewed the settlers who built a small home, planted crops, and raised a few domesticated animals. Imagine how it must have looked to the Comanches to see early Texans bringing in herds of cattle when there were already immense herds of buffalo.

Settlements, Missions, and Forts

For the settlers, owning one's own piece of land, however humble, was the dream of a lifetime. This lifestyle was one way in which the Native Americans and the settlers simply could not understand each other.

To the west of this land, where settlers and adventurers began to wander, were the mountains; to the east, the timber; and to the south, the hot, dry savannas and the sea. The territory was a rich land of plateaus and prairies, hills and valleys. Incredibly fertile, the land drew huge herds of buffalo. Herds numbered in the millions.

This enormous land was part of New Spain, the northern reaches of a land colonized by the Spaniards just as the thirteen American colonies had been settled mostly by the English. Yet, unlike the Spanish lands in Mexico, this northern area had few Spanish settlements, forts, or missions.

Texas has an extremely varied terrain. It includes hills, mountains, woods, and desert, and borders the Gulf of Mexico.

The missions, founded by well-meaning Spanish priests who wanted to make Catholics of the Native Americans, did not enjoy the great success the padres had hoped for. The Lipan Apaches and the Comanches generally ignored the efforts of the missionaries, and instead occasionally raided their ranches and farms. Other tribes, especially the mild Coahuiltecans, did flock to the missions. They learned Spanish and Christian ways. But some found the rules and regulations, the stern doses of a new religion, and the regimented lifestyle hard to accept. Some left; many more died from new European illnesses such as smallpox and measles. The missions and their inhabitants struggled against many obstacles.

To protect the missions, the Spanish often built forts, called presidios. Manned by soldiers who were ill-equipped and often not even paid, the presidios were no challenge to the Comanches. Conditions were getting worse, not better, in this territory for the missionaries and the soldiers.

In the 1760s, the king of Spain sent the Marqués de Rubí to map this vast area all the way to the Pacific Ocean. Rubí sent back a recommendation that the Spanish should give up trying to tame the land, and simply pull back, leaving this great land to "Nature and the Indians."[2]

THE EAGLE AND THE CACTUS

Spain, of course, did not give back the land. It held control of the region, part of the enormous prize that Hernando Cortés had conquered. Conditions for everyone but the ruling Spaniards were appalling. All but the very top level of society lived in poverty, and political repression was total.

After a long and bloody struggle that began in 1810, Mexico won its independence from Spain in 1821. A colorful eccentric named Agustin Iturbide declared himself emperor, occupying what he called the "throne of Moctezuma."[1] Only two years later, Brigadier General Antonio López de Santa Anna helped overthrow Iturbide and declare the new country of Mexico a republic to be based on liberal principles. For the common person in Mexico, conditions under Spanish colonial rule had been bad. Now they were even worse.

The flag of the new Mexican nation was tri-colored, formed by broad green, white, and red vertical stripes. In the center, against the white background, was the national symbol—an eagle perched on a cactus with a snake in its beak. In ancient Aztec days, when the tribe wandered without an area that they could call their own, one of their myths was that when they saw an eagle perched on a cactus with a snake in its mouth they would have found the perfect place to settle. The story tells that they did, indeed, see the eagle and the snake at the place where present-day Mexico City is located, and on that spot, the ancient Aztecs built their capitol.

Wealth, Poverty, and Political Chaos

Because of the chaos of years of bloody fighting, the people were even poorer than they had been. Economic conditions were in disarray, and one military group after another gained temporary control

The Mexican Flag is green, white, and red. An eagle with a snake in its beak is perched on a cactus in the center of the flag.

of the country. Everyone thought that once the Spanish rulers were thrown out everything would improve. They were wrong. Ironically, it would take fifty years to gain back even the bad conditions that had existed before they won their independence.

The gap between rich and poor, already vast under Spanish rule, became greater. The roots of this discrepancy had always been racial—Spaniards born in Spain were at the very top level; Spaniards born in New Spain a bit lower; the new group called *mestizos* (people of mixed blood) were on the next rung down; and the Native Americans were at the very bottom.

A rich woman, when asked why she rode everywhere in her carriage, setting foot on the pavement only to saunter into one of the luxurious shops that catered to the rich, answered, "After all, everybody has feet, but only ladies have carriages." Ladies, she continued, avoided "profaning the soles of their feet by contact with their mother earth."[2]

On the other hand, the majority of the people had plenty of contact with their mother earth because most floors in the hovels in which they lived, hungry and poor, were made of dirt.

Mexico City teemed with beggars and day laborers scrounging for whatever employment that they could find. As bad as conditions were in the city, more and more people flocked there because life in the countryside was even worse.

In 1828, a Tribunal for Vagrants was created in Mexico City to give the appearance of legality to the act of taking men against their will and putting them in the army. On a single night, five hundred men were arrested and signed up in the army simply because they were found in *cantinas*—cheap bars where they could drown their sorrows for a few pesos. These men hardly made the most devoted soldiers.

For the poor foot soldier, the army was just another way in which they were exploited by the rich. But for upper-class men, joining the army could be a pathway to great power and riches. Because it was an opportunity to steal without consequences, being an army officer could be a way to become wealthy.

Partly for this reason, the Mexican Army was composed of eighty thousand men; it took up 80 percent of public spending and it had many more officers than an army that size really needs.[3]

Santa Anna

In contrast to the poverty of the country was the dashing military figure of Antonio López de Santa Anna. Becoming president of Mexico in 1832, he was also commander of the army. Santa Anna grew up in the town of Jalapa in the mountains west of the port of Veracruz.[4] His father was a respected businessperson. The family was mostly—but not entirely—of Spanish descent, with little Native American blood.

General Antonio López de Santa Anna was president of Mexico eleven times. He led the Mexican Army in its attack of the Alamo.

Although Santa Anna was always dedicated to the glory of Mexico, he was even more dedicated to his own glory. He gained a reputation for being unstable, greedy, and vain. In those chaotic years when a man who commanded an army could rise to power overnight, Santa Anna proved himself one of the smartest and most energetic of leaders. As a young man, he wangled a commission in the army and quickly proved his military skill. His position would gain him enormous power.

As powerful as Santa Anna was, his country was still in chaos. His government paid little attention to the vast empty land to the north.

Moses Austin's Plan

It was in this almost empty land in the north of Mexico, with warring Comanches and Apaches riding freely, that an American named Moses Austin planned to settle.

For years before he even thought of immigrating to Mexico, Moses Austin had been a successful lead miner and banker in the United States. In 1818, however, the United States entered one of its periodic economic crashes—land values plummeted and banks failed—and Moses Austin looked around for better opportunities. Why not Mexico? In that big, empty land, Austin speculated, there would be undreamed of opportunities.

Moses Austin, a Missouri banker, asked the Spanish government in San Antonio to allow him to bring Americans to settle there.

Moses Austin wanted to make a special deal with the Spanish government. (It wouldn't be until February 1821 that Mexico would secure independence from Spain.) He wanted to bring a group of American families into the Texas country. But the powerful man in charge of the area, General Joaquin Arredondo, had made a career of stamping out American settlers. He saw the few who had managed to settle as trouble-makers, and he gave orders that no *Norte americanos* were allowed to enter.

Moses Austin, exhausted after his eight hundred-mile trip on horseback, rode into San Antonio de Bexar (present-day San Antonio, Texas, where the Alamo is located) in the winter of 1820 to plead his case.

Before the Spaniards, Austin made three points: First, the Comanches were still dangerous, and they would continue to be a problem for the government until the area was settled. Second, no Mexican settlers were coming into the area. In fact, more were leaving it. Third, Austin convinced them that there was simply no other way to colonize the area.

The American settlers would be a buffer between Mexican settlements to the south and the marauding tribes to the north. Thus, they would tend to keep out the wild adventurers and vagabonds who had given them so much trouble in the past.

The government agreed to let Austin bring American settlers into Texas, but it set up tough standards about who would be allowed to come: They had to have "good character and habits . . . and . . . be obedient in all things to the government . . . and faithful."[5] They had to agree, too, to become Catholics and citizens. Austin, however, made it clear that the demand that the settlers become Catholics would not be enforced too strictly. Besides, hardly any priests were assigned to cover the new colonists. In fact, almost none of the settlers converted.

Moses Austin rode out of San Antonio de Bexar in January 1821 to take the good news back to Missouri. He had to cross long stretches of the wildest country on the frontier. He ran out of food, was robbed, and got sick. He arrived in Missouri barely alive. On his deathbed, he pleaded with his son Stephen to promise to lead the settlers into Texas.

Stephen Austin and the Old Three Hundred

Stephen Austin was twenty-seven years old. He had already been to the best private schools in Connecticut, graduating from Transylvania College in Kentucky. As a teenager, he was elected to the Territorial Legislature of Missouri and became a director of his father's bank. Later he was appointed as a territorial circuit judge.

He and his father both had lost most of their money in the financial ups and downs of the American economy. As much as any of the other settlers, he was ready for a new life, whatever the risks.

Off he rode into the huge, hostile land that was to become Texas, looking for the ideal spot to lead his

Stephen Austin followed through on his father's dream of leading Americans to colonize Texas.

crop of the first three hundred families of settlers. He was given the freedom to choose where to settle with his followers—who would come to be called the Old Three Hundred—as long as he did not wander too far south.

Stephen Austin found exactly what he was looking for in the rich river bottoms between the Colorado River and the Brazos River. With abundant rainfall and access to the gulf, this was prime farmland. It was, he wrote in a letter, "as good in every respect as man could wish for, land first rate, plenty of timber, fine water—beautifully rolling."[6]

The first settler to enter Austin's colony was Andrew Robinson, who crossed the Brazos in

November 1821. Perhaps he was impressed with how hard it was to get across the river, because he stayed right there, seeing an opportunity for a business. He somehow got hold of a boat and started to operate a ferry.

Other settlers rapidly followed. In January 1822, Jared E. Groce—a planter, lumberman, and capitalist from Georgia—rolled into Texas with fifty wagons and ninety African-American slaves.[7]

The Mexican government agreed to give more land to those who planned to raise stock, since they needed wide open spaces to graze their animals. So even people who wanted only to farm put themselves down as cattle ranchers. Also, since a family was granted much more land than a single person, some twenty-six family grants were given to bachelors who joined together in twos and threes to create a "family" and satisfy the letter of the law. These early settlers chose some of the best farming land to be had.

The Mexican government had laid down some strict laws of behavior for the colonists, but Stephen Austin's rules for conduct were even more stern. He forbade any "frontiersman who has no other occupation than that of hunter," and "no drunkard, no gambler, no profane swearer, no idler."[8] Austin made sure that the rules were enforced, and he drove several families out for breaking them.

The first year was arduous. Drought ruined the first crops, and the Karankawa tribe of Native Americans (another warring group in the area) attacked and killed a large number of settlers. Some families, disillusioned with the harsh conditions, went back to an easier life in the United States. Gradually, however, conditions did improve.

Farming, livestock, and some hunting provided food for the settlers, and before long there was a thriving economy. With almost no money available, most businesses were based on barter. The books of an early merchant, George Erath, show an intricate listing of goods balanced against other goods: clothing traded for hogs, horses exchanged for corn, an ox for a sow, a feather bed for three cows with calves, and a gun for a mare.[9]

Over the next ten years, Austin brought in a total of fifteen hundred families, and soon more land grants were made to more groups of settlers. In a single decade, these settlers cleared more land, put in more crops, had more children, and built more towns than the Spanish had in three hundred years.

These settlers were tough, motivated, resourceful Americans—even if they had sworn allegiance to Mexico. As children they had learned to shoot their hunting rifles. Most of the women were as able to pick up a rifle and take aim as well as the men. Day by day and year by year, after the Old Three Hundred, more and more rugged settlers and footloose adventurers poured into this new land.

The summer of 1835 was a turning point in the story of the Alamo and all of Texas. The majority of Texans were still in favor of peace and loyalty to the independent country of Mexico.[1] They were

THE TEXAS REVOLUTION

farmers and ranchers who just wanted to get on with their lives, plant their crops, and tend their herds.

Many of the people living in Texas were men and women who had come from a true democracy. The brutal dictatorship of Santa Anna and the threatened loss of their freedoms was very significant. Much like the American colonists in the years leading up to the American Revolution in 1776, these early Texans had become used to living far from the center of government and running their own affairs. They were willing to be Mexican citizens technically if it was to their advantage, but not if they had to obey dictatorial rules made in a far-off capital.

Talk began of open rebellion against Mexico—at first to defend the freedoms of the Mexican Constitution of 1824 (the constitution written after Mexico gained its freedom from Spain), and then to declare that Texas was to be a free and independent republic itself. There had been a few shots fired between settlers and Mexican troops, but serious armed conflict started in the summer of 1835. The tiny town of Gonzalez had a small cannon. The cannon was not much use in real fighting and crudely mounted on some wheels made of slices of tree trunk, but it was still capable of making a grand noise to frighten off the Comanches. Captain Francisco Castaneda of the Mexican Army was sent to Gonzales in September 1835 with orders to capture the cannon.

"Come and Take It"

In a defiant mood, two local women—Sarah Seeley and Evaline DeWitt—made a flag out of DeWitt's wedding dress. On it they printed the challenge "Come and Take It." Almeron Dickinson, a former artilleryman in the United States Army, fired the little cannon at the Mexican Army. Ever after, Texans have called this "The First Shot of The Texas Revolution."[2] The Mexicans never did capture the cannon.

After a few skirmishes with Mexican troops, the Texans decided to set up their own government. In November 1835, the settlers and Sam Houston gathered at San Felipe and decided to elect a governor, Henry Smith. The main order of business was to form armed resistance against the Mexicans—that was clear—and they needed a strong leader to take charge. Houston willingly stepped into that role for his fellow settlers, and they just as willingly followed him. He was the perfect man to organize and lead a fighting force for the Texans.

"Santa Anna's Mistake"

Mexican president Santa Anna heard of the armed resistance and sent his brother-in-law Martin Perfect de Cos north with an army. Santa Anna voided the liberal Mexican Constitution of 1824 and set up a powerful central government, giving himself un-limited power. He announced that, henceforth, taxes and customs collections would be part of Texas life. All decisions affecting Texan lives would be made far to the south in Mexico City.

Stephen Austin, who had gone to Mexico City a year and a half earlier to try to work out some prob-lems with the government, had been tossed into jail. He had been there ever since, and when he was re-leased, he returned to Texas. Eighteen months in a Mexican jail had left him with little faith that Texas could remain Mexican.

Santa Anna interpreted the presence of even a few hotheads in Texas as a serious threat and ordered Cos to get tough. General Cos ordered the arrest of several troublemakers, including William Barret Travis—a popular figure among the settlers. Reaction was swift and fiery. People banded together to form what they called "committees for public safety."[3]

Santa Anna placed Cos in charge of the situation in Texas. Although the Mexican military had many brave and skilled officers, Martin Perfect de Cos was not one of them. His chief claim to power and authority was that he was married to Santa Anna's sister. When he was put in charge of the Mexican

Army in Texas, he was put in a job for which he was totally unsuited. He started north, blustering about how he was going to teach the upstart foreigners a lesson.

General Cos arrived and occupied San Antonio and the Alamo. Through a series of botched opportunities and glaring military mistakes, Cos lost San Antonio and the Alamo on December 11, 1835, to a ragtag Texas force led by Edward Burleson and Benjamin Milam.[4] It was a humiliating defeat, and Cos was forced to promise to leave Texas and never fight against the Texans again.

When Cos returned to Mexico, Santa Anna was enraged. He had not chosen well—Cos was no leader. The Texans had been fortunate in that they had several brave, smart, and strong leaders, including Sam Houston and Jim Bowie.

Sam Houston

Sam Houston was the only man ever to serve as governor of two states, Tennessee and Texas. After Texas won independence from Mexico, he was also president of the Republic of Texas for two terms, then a United States Senator from the state of Texas after it was admitted to the Union. A big strong man in a land of big strong men, he was a dramatic dresser, often mixing Cherokee, Mexican, Arab, and European clothing styles. An astute politician and diplomat, Houston was one of the authentic giants of American history.

Born in Virginia in 1793, Houston was raised by his soon widowed mother, who took his nine brothers and sisters to Tennessee. Houston was still very young when he decided that he wanted to live with the Cherokees. He loved them and they loved him, dubbing him "the Raven." The Cherokees accepted Houston as one of them. He developed a lifelong respect for Native Americans and an understanding of their problems, even when it made his own life more difficult.

In 1818, after witnessing President Andrew Jackson's policy of taking Native American land at gunpoint and forcing tribes to move great distances to live in poverty on reservations, Houston renounced his commission in the army.

In the fight for Texan independence, Sam Houston played a leading role. He was president of the Republic of Texas for two terms. He also served as governor and senator of the state.

Elected to Congress in 1823, Houston was then elected governor of Tennessee in 1827. He married Eliza Allen in 1829, when he was thirty-four years old and she was still in her teens. Within a few months, Eliza had left him, returning to her parents. Neither Sam nor Eliza ever revealed the reason, but the townspeople speculated that the separation was Houston's fault.

Houston then gave up his position as governor and headed to Arkansas to live with the Cherokees. Later, Houston went to Washington, D.C., to try to get President Jackson to protect the Cherokee people, but he failed. Jackson suggested that he go to Texas to negotiate with Native American tribes who were carrying out raids into United States territory. Houston wrote back to the president, calling Texas "the finest country to its extent upon the globe."[5]

In November 1835, when the settlers and Houston gathered at San Felipe and elected Henry Smith as governor, Texas was still a part of Mexico. It was not clear to anybody exactly what Smith was to govern, but the main order of business was to form armed resistance against the Mexicans. Sam Houston was the perfect man to organize and lead a fighting force for the Texans.

James Bowie

In 1836, James Bowie went to the Alamo to look over the place and to make an important decision—whether or not to blow it up. As a fortification, the old mission could be as useful to the Mexican Army as it could be to the Texans. Bowie stayed on with the few men who were still there and wrote Houston that they would defend the place.

James Bowie was born in 1786.[6] As a young man, he was known to be rash and he often got into trouble. By 1836, Bowie was already one of the best known and most colorful of America's frontiersmen, and he was to play an important role in the coming conflict.

Bowie came from a family who committed rash acts. In Georgia, his father was once sent to jail for murder. On the night he was arrested, Bowie's mother, with the help of a slave, broke him out of jail, and they fled to Louisiana with six-year-old Jim tagging along. Since Louisiana was still in the hands of the French, the renegade family was out of reach of the law.

Bowie grew up tough, a skilled fighter and a man to be dealt with in a time and a world where disputes were often settled with fists, knives, and guns. But the young Bowie also gained a reputation for being generous and open-hearted, courteous to men and women. He was a good friend, but a fierce enemy.

His line of work would not be considered proper today. He made a fortune smuggling slaves and cheating people in land deals. Bowie bought goods from the notorious pirate Jean Lafitte's raids and sold them at a profit.

Jim Bowie was a colorful frontiersman, who became a legendary hero of the Texas Revolution.

Bowie became a famous knife duelist. In one fight, he slew three men with a weapon bigger and more deadly than anyone had ever seen. As the story of "Bowie's knife" spread, thousands of people across the country clamored to have one like it. Who actually designed and made the original? Stories vary—it may have been Bowie's brother Rezin, or perhaps an Arkansas blacksmith named James Black. Whoever it was, the Bowie knife entered the pages of Western lore.

As the eastern parts of the United States grew too crowded and too tame for Bowie, he headed to Texas—a magnet for adventurers. He settled in San Antonio.

Bowie converted to Catholicism in order to marry Ursula de Veramendi, daughter of the lieutenant governor of Texas, and accepted Mexican citizenship. Before long, he had obtained seven hundred fifty thousand acres of land.

Bowie seems to have been as close to a model citizen as he could be expected to be. He and his wife had two children, and Bowie's fortunes grew. He was involved in land speculating and prospecting schemes. Fluent in Spanish, he got along well with the Mexicans of San Antonio, and with the new Texans who arrived from the United States.

Then tragedy struck. A cholera epidemic swept the area, and his wife and two children died suddenly.

In an earlier duel, Bowie had been pierced by a sword cane in his left lung. He developed a chronic upper respiratory problem, which in those days would probably have been treated with alcohol—to help the lungs clear.

Along with many other Americans who fought in the Texas Revolution, Bowie was technically a Mexican citizen, and therefore, considered a traitor to the land of his recently sworn allegiance. It was very similar to the situation of the American Revolution against England. The men and women who fought in that Revolution were English citizens who were called traitors by King George of England. Mexicans who fought for freedom against Spain were also called traitors. Now the Texans were called the same name by Mexico.

There was no doubt in Bowie's mind where his loyalty lay. As soon as the fighting started, he accepted a commission as a colonel in the Texas army to fight against Mexico.

As 1836 grew nearer, Bowie became more and more ill. Historians are not sure exactly what illness he suffered from. Whatever the illness, it was serious enough to weaken this big, strong fighting man.

As Bowie surveyed and prepared the few ill-equipped stragglers who had nothing else to do but hang around the Alamo, a powerful opposing fighting force, led by General Santa Anna, began marching north.

Santa Anna's Army

Santa Anna did not want to have to put down this ragtag rebellion. He had already sent another man to do the job. It was at least partly because of the fiasco of General Cos that Santa Anna was so determined to show no mercy to the Texans who held the Alamo.

He gathered thousands of troops and marched north. He was not going to give up such a huge chunk of Mexico to these people he often referred to as "pirates." This was Mexico—his country, his laws—and these people had promised to be loyal Mexican citizens. They were betraying their promises and were traitors.

Santa Anna knew of the many stories that had already begun to be told about him, eventually making him almost a mythic figure. Historians agree that some of the stories are true; some, partly true; and surely others were made up. Santa Anna himself encouraged the legend.[7]

One story tells that, in disguise, Santa Anna attended Washington's Birthday Ball in San Antonio the night before his army arrived in town to begin the siege of the Alamo. The tale claims that he danced with the ladies and drank tequila, enjoying himself and picking up valuable information. This story, while amusing, seems very unlikely.

There were several people at that party who had met Santa Anna and would have seen through any disguise. In fact, had he arrived that night, he probably could have taken the Alamo almost single-handedly since all but ten Texans were carousing at the party!

The army that General Santa Anna led north was a fighting force to be reckoned with, made up of veterans and recruits. The best *soldados* (soldiers) had served, putting down various rebellious groups within Mexico, over the last five years.

Most of the Mexican soldiers had been forced into the army. Unlike the United States, Mexico used the draft system to fill up the ranks. A recruiting officer of the period wrote to his superior: "Here are 300 volunteers. I will send you 300 more if you return the chains."[8] This was how most of the men who marched north with Santa Anna were "recruited" into the army.

But when the time for a battle came, experience had shown that they were not bad fighters. Submissive and used to obeying orders, these Mexican soldiers took to military training without too much trouble. They could be worked up to make a good charge, but were less effective in defense.

These Mexican soldiers were small but tough and usually hardy men, averaging seven inches shorter than the Texans. On the rugged march north, the weaker soldiers gave up and only the strongest reached Texas. In his haste, Santa Anna had neglected to bring any doctors with his army and almost every Mexican fighting soldier who was seriously wounded died.

The firearms that the Mexicans carried north with them were mostly muskets, a simple weapon that had been in use a hundred years before. It fired only once without being reloaded, and even for trained soldiers, the musket was slow to reload. Usually the soldiers charged forward firing their muskets from the hip and then fought at close quarters with bayonets.

Only a few Mexican soldiers had rifles, a weapon only then coming into use in armies. Although it could still only be loaded one shot at a time, a rifle was superior in the hands of a skilled shooter. Muskets had smooth bores and were less accurate. Rifles had spiral grooves (called rifling) in the barrel, which set a bullet spinning, making it much more likely to hit the target.

Santa Anna's artillery (cannon) consisted of twenty-one guns. He had with him four-pounders, six-pounders, eight-pounders, and twelve-pounders. The numbers referred not to the weight of the gun, but to how much the cannon ball weighed. For battering down thick walls, only the twelve-pounders would do much good.

Santa Anna had with him another deadly piece of artillery, the howitzer. Howitzers lofted small bombs, usually over the walls of a fort, to blow up the inside.

While Santa Anna's troops advanced, preparations were made inside the Alamo. This photograph, taken in 1907, shows the interior of the Alamo.

Artillery was used in battle in another, more ruthless way in those days. Firing a single blast of grape-shot—dozens of small chunks of metal—from a cannon could rip apart several of the enemy. Often a cannon was aimed at the hard, rocky ground in front of advancing troops so that all those deadly pieces of metal would bounce and scatter into the thick of the enemy.

Some of the officers who led these soldiers were often not much better trained than their troops. The Mexican Army was top-heavy, with far more officers than it needed. Four times larger than the Texas army, it had thirty-three times more generals.[9]

Because many of his soldiers and his officers were poorly trained, Santa Anna always made very careful plans for battle. He left as little as possible to the initiative of his troops and their officers. While Santa Anna's army continued to march north, the Texans in the Alamo prepared for battle.

5 ★

THE CALM BEFORE THE STORM

Some of the confusion in getting the Alamo ready to ward off Santa Anna's impending attack was due to the conflict between two men with different personalities— James Bowie and William Barret Travis.

Travis (1809–1836) was from South Carolina, and was a former school teacher and lawyer.[1] He had moved to Alabama, married, became a lawyer, then abandoned his wife and child to head for Texas. According to a story later handed down in his family, Travis killed a man and had to leave.

Bowie vs. Travis—A Struggle for Command

Travis settled in San Felipe de Austin, a small town northeast of the Alamo. There he practiced law and began spending much of his time in the company of various women. The idea of the Texas Revolution appealed to him, and he was soon given a command as lieutenant colonel in the barely formed Texas Cavalry Corps.

Bowie and James C. Neill were at the Alamo when Travis arrived. Sent to reinforce the Alamo, Travis

William Barret Travis was one hero of the battle of the Alamo. He was a courageous and devoted leader.

was ready to fight and die. He was six feet tall and weighed 175 pounds. There was a bit too much of the spit-and-polish military attitude in his bearing, but no one doubted his courage and devotion to his troops and he commanded a sometimes grudging respect.

Unfortunately, Lieutenant Colonel Neill left the Alamo for a twenty-five-day furlough on February 13. Travis, a very formal soldier, and Bowie, rough and ready with no desire to follow orders, butted heads.

Bowie felt that since he was fourteen years older than Travis and he was Sam Houston's personal representative here, he outranked him.

Most of the Texans, in an impromptu election, chose Bowie to command the town and Travis to command the Alamo. The two men then came to a compromise in order not to have two conflicting groups: Travis would command all the regular soldiers and the cavalry (loosely defined as anyone with a horse), and Bowie would be in charge of the volunteers. When Neill returned he could run the whole show.

Half-horse, Half-alligator

Then Davy Crockett arrived with fourteen men, an informal militia that banded together to ride off to adventure with their charismatic leader.

This leader, called "half-horse, half-alligator," was the tale-spinning, fiddle-playing, joke-cracking frontiersman, David Crockett (1786–1836).[2] Davy Crockett was among the most famous of the colorful characters of the American West. Generations of children grew up on his stories. Familiar still is the larger-than-life image of Crockett with his coonskin cap and the rifle that he called "Old Betsy."

With little—as he would have called it—book learning, he was very well educated in the ways of the woods. He did spend six months in school once to impress a young woman, but dropped out when she rejected him.[3] Aside from that, he had no patience for sitting in a schoolroom.

As a young man, Crockett volunteered to fight under the leadership of Andrew Jackson in a war against the Creek tribe of Native Americans. He did not fight long, upset by the horrible offenses committed by the United States Army. Crockett understood Native

Americans and was sympathetic to their problems. He campaigned many times against the practice of taking their lands away from them against their will and forcing them to march long distances to be relocated on often barren reservations.

Crockett took up farming, married, and fathered three children. When his wife died, he mourned her for a short while and then married a young widow and added her two children to his brood.

He was a terrible farmer and lost money in several business ventures. His winning personality, however, helped him become a state legislator from 1821 to 1825.

Crockett loved being referred to as "half-horse, half-alligator." His true fame came from this wild reputation, and from the stories of his adventures. He disappeared for long stretches of time, wandering off in the woods and writing fanciful tales about his escapades.

No one doubts that Davy Crockett was a mighty hunter, but some find it hard to believe his claim of killing 108 bears in an eight-month period. In 1835, he made a triumphal tour of eastern cities, where he was famous for his stories and for the stories others had written about him. He was a man of high spirits and rich laughter.

When he was beaten in a reelection bid to the United States Congress, he informed the voters: "You may all go to Hell. And I will go to Texas."[4] He wrote, "I promise to give the Texans a helping hand on the high road to freedom."

Davy Crockett boosted the morale of the men at the Alamo when he volunteered to fight alongside them against Santa Anna's army.

And he did, riding off toting his famous fiddle. In the words of one historian, Crockett "rode to the scent of trouble."[5]

The wide open spaces of Texas inspired Crockett. From San Augustine, Texas, he had written back to his family on January 9, 1836: "I expect in all probability to settle on the Bodark or Chocktaw Bayou or Red River, that I have no doubt is the richest country in the world, good land, plenty of timber, and the best springs. . . . I am rejoiced at my fate. . . . I am in great hopes of making a fortune for myself and family."[6]

Some historians wonder if Crockett had in mind even more than good land and fortune. He expected the Texans to win in their conflict with Mexico. As a hero of that struggle he might even have hoped to become President Crockett—not president of the Republic of Texas, but of the United States.

He gave the morale of the defenders in the Alamo a boost when he rode in. His stories, his fiddle, and his gregarious and charming personality won over everyone. He even seemed to get along just fine with Travis, a man whose strict military attitude could get on the nerves of free-spirited pioneers. In a letter smuggled out of the walls, he wrote of Travis: "He will have snakes to eat before he [Santa Anna] gets over the wall, I tell you."[7]

Santa Anna Advances

At a party given to celebrate Crockett's arrival, news arrived that Santa Anna was much closer and had a bigger army than anyone had imagined possible. One report put the number of his troops at an improbable thirteen thousand—others said more like five thousand.

Although Santa Anna's huge army was little more than a two-day march from the Alamo, neither Travis nor Bowie did much to make last-minute preparations. A lookout was posted in a church tower, but the leaders neglected to call all the people into the Alamo. They also did not do much to bring in supplies such as food and firewood.

Historians wonder why better preparations were not made. One of the possible answers is that after the fairly easy defeat of General Cos just a month before, the Texans did not believe that they had much to fear from the Mexican Army. They also could have felt that Santa Anna would take quite a while to reach them. It should be remembered too that, although many of the soldiers in the Alamo had experience fighting Native American war parties, they lacked the seasoning gained from doing battle with a large and well-organized army.

The Mexican Army moved steadily north as quickly as Santa Anna could move them over the desolate landscape. It was one of the worst marches that the Mexican Army had ever experienced.

Santa Anna knew, as did Mexican generals before him, that the easiest way to invade Texas was by sea. Ships could arrive in the small ports along the gulf, allowing troops to strike quickly into Texas. But a fleet would take time to gather and organize, and Santa Anna felt that quick action was necessary.

So his army marched north across great stretches of empty and inhospitable land. In his haste, Santa Anna had supplied his army poorly, with little food for the long march and no medical supplies.

Frigid winter winds blew down from the north into the face of his advancing army. Although the army averaged fifteen to twenty miles per day of hard marching, many soldiers died along the way.

As they marched, they encountered not one but two of the most daunting blasts of weather imaginable: "Blue Northers." A Blue Norther, which is rare in Texan winters, is a very strong cold front that flows from Canada southward across the Plains. Even today, Texans remark that there is not much between the North Pole and Texas except barbed wire. This awesome blast of wind from the frozen north can cause the temperature to drop twenty to thirty degrees within an hour.

The Blue Norther comes with icy rain and sleet and sometimes even snow. It gained its unusual name because, as it approaches, a distinct blue line darkens the normal color of the sky. The sight of this blue line was a death sentence for many Mexican soldiers.

Especially vulnerable were the troops from the hotter areas of Mexico. They had no winter clothes, many were barefoot, and they were not used to cold weather. Many fell back, already weakened from hunger and long days of marching, to shiver and die. Santa Anna continued onward, seeking glory for Mexico.

In spite of the warnings, the Mexican general's arrival was something of a surprise. No one expected him to march north into the teeth of winter. Even if he did something so rash, no one expected him so soon.

With less than two hundred soldiers and no promise of reinforcements, Travis, Bowie, and Crockett knew that they could not hope to defend the town of San Antonio itself. When word came that Santa Anna's arrival was imminent, they moved quickly within the walls of the Alamo.

Last-Minute Preparations

Although it may not have been spoken this early in the siege, the Texans who rushed inside must have known that it was only a matter of time. They could put up a good fight, they could die bravely—but without a large number of reinforcements, they could not hope to win. And yet, with the vast open prairie beckoning in every direction but south, no one fled . . . at least, not yet. There was blustering talk, with Crockett, Bowie, and Travis encouraging the troops. But no one was fooled. The situation looked very bad.

The Alamo

What came to be known as the "Alamo" started out as a Catholic mission made up of a granary, convento (priest quarters), workshops, quarters for the converted Native Americans, corrals, gardens, and the church. The mission was named San Antonio de Valero and was founded on the west bank of the San Antonio River in 1718.[8]

That site was abandoned in favor of a new site on the east bank of the river. The temporary buildings erected there were destroyed by a hurricane in 1724. The mission site was again moved and work at the present site started. The first stone church on the new site collapsed, and in 1756, work on the present church began. It was never finished. In 1793, Mission Valero was secularized—closed to missionary work. Its lands and buildings were either given to the remaining Native American families or sold. The

Catholic Church retained the unfinished church and convento.

Mission Valero became known as the "Alamo" when a detachment of troops were sent north from a post in Mexico called *Pueblo de San Carlos del Alamo de Parras*, "Alamo" for short. When they were posted at the old mission, the troops called it the "Alamo," in nostalgic memory of the spot from where they came. The name stuck.

Over the years, additional buildings were erected and walls added, ending up with more or less what

This diorama shows how the Alamo looked at the time of the battle.

one can see in illustrations and maps. "More or less" applies because no two surviving plans seem to be exactly the same. The area was roughly two acres, with the walls and structures in place by 1811.

The Alamo had been built originally as a mission. In spite of the forty years it had served as a military fortification, it still lacked even basic necessities for defense.

The tops of the walls had no parapets—stone mini-walls behind which a soldier could stand and fire. There were also no bastions—structures that jut out and allow defenders to fire to the sides at enemies trying to scale the walls. Another problem was that the outer perimeter was just too long for the number of soldiers available to properly defend it.

General Cos's troops had started the military work in 1835. They had hastily built rough parapets and placed a log-and-earth wall at the south end of the grounds, where there had been no wall at all. The Texans worked to improve these fortifications and erect new ones where needed. If the defenders had been concentrated in a much smaller fort, with proper parapets, bastions, and thick walls, they could have hoped to hold out longer.

The defenders knocked holes in the interior walls of the buildings so that they could move about freely, if and when the attackers made it over the walls. Supplies were hurriedly brought in at the last minute—some corn and a few cattle. An old well was cleared out and opened, but no one had thought to

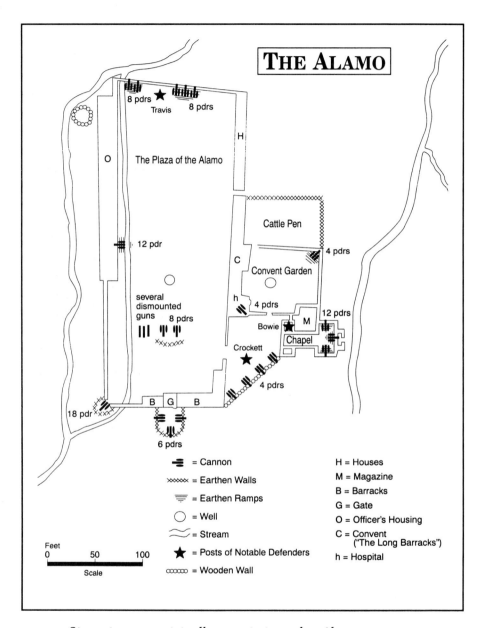

THE ALAMO

8 pdrs
Travis
8 pdrs

H

O

The Plaza of the Alamo

Cattle Pen

12 pdr

4 pdrs

C

Convent Garden

several
dismounted
guns   8 pdrs

h

4 pdrs

12 pdrs

M

Bowie

Chapel

Crockett

4 pdrs

18 pdr

B G B

6 pdrs

≡ = Cannon

xxxxx = Earthen Walls

≡ = Earthen Ramps

○ = Well

〜 = Stream

★ = Posts of Notable Defenders

ccccc = Wooden Wall

H = Houses

M = Magazine

B = Barracks

G = Gate

O = Officer's Housing

C = Convent
("The Long Barracks")

h = Hospital

Feet
0   50   100

Scale

Since it was originally a mission, the Alamo was not intended to be used as a fort. The men inside the Alamo hastily prepared for its defense by placing cannon in strategic positions.

bring in enough firewood for cooking and for warmth during the icy nights. Another task that they had neglected to do was to clear the land around the fortification of trees, bushes, and even small shacks that could provide cover for the attackers.

Ammunition was in very short supply. Always resourceful, the Texans melted down the lead that surrounded many of the windows in town and made musket balls. They also chopped up horseshoes, chains, and other bits of metal to provide the deadly grapeshot that their cannon would belch out at the attackers.

The Texans' artillery, about twenty cannon, was placed in what Travis and Bowie thought were the best spots. They were mostly mounted on the walls, facing the open spaces that the enemy would have to cross. For the bigger cannon that lacked proper carriages, improvised piles of dirt had to do.

One of the fort's gunners was a man named Captain Almeron Dickinson. He helped place the various cannon, even placing some inside the walls. These pointed at the inside of the main gate and the inside of the hastily constructed wood-and-earth wall. Even if the Mexicans broke through, they would be faced with more deadly cannon fire.

What is not clear from the historical records is whether or not Dickinson thought to pre-sight his guns at various points outside the walls so that he would not have to do it during the attack. Pre-sighting cannon at spots where defenders expect attackers to appear can save time during battle and make the cannon fire much more effective.

Every soldier had a musket or rifle, and fortunately, many were crack shots. Many carried sidearms and knives as well. Even if they could not win—or even survive—the Texan defenders would make sure that the battle was a bloody one.

The one real hope that Travis, Bowie, Crockett, and the other defenders had was for reinforcements to arrive. Letter after letter was dispatched, carried by men on fast horses who managed to sneak through the Mexican lines. Plea after plea was sent to the outside world for more soldiers, more ammunition—for more hope.

It is here that one of the most interesting and puzzling characters of the story of the Alamo must be introduced.

James Fannin Walker

James Fannin Walker (1804–1836) was born in Georgia, the son of a doctor and a young aristocratic woman. He was raised by his mother's grandmother.[9]

He made it into West Point, where officers of the United States Army were (and still are) trained. He did not enjoy being a member of the military, and he resigned two years later. When he left, he stood sixtieth in a class of eighty-six. He changed his name to James Fannin and hoped for a new life.

Fannin married and in 1834, moved to Texas. There he became a successful land speculator and slave trader. He advertised his slaves as all having "Congo accents,"[10] which told buyers that they were direct from Africa and supposedly better workers. This was at a time when it was legal to own slaves, but no longer legal to bring them from Africa.

As he prospered, Fannin began to support the cause of Texas independence. He fought several times in the various skirmishes against Mexico.

During the siege of the Alamo, Fannin was holed up in Goliad—a small village about eighty miles southeast of the Alamo—with between four hundred and four hundred fifty fighting soldiers and a fair amount of supplies. Indecisive at first in response to Travis's pleas, he finally acted. He loaded up some wagons, got his troops together, and headed for the Alamo.

A few hundred yards down the trail, still within sight of Goliad, some of his wagons broke. He took this as a sign that his mission was hopeless, and headed back to safety.[11]

Would Fannin's presence at the Alamo have tipped the balance in favor of the Texans? The answer, historians say, must almost certainly be no—but nobody will ever know for sure. It finally became clear to the defenders that Fannin would not be coming to help—that nobody would be there in time to help defend the Alamo.

THE BLOCKADE

This moment was the true test of the—take your pick—bravery or foolhardiness of the defenders. It also gave rise to one of the most colorful moments in the history of Texas.

The Mexican Army Arrives

Whatever the rest of the people under Travis's command could be called—foolhardy, foolish, too brave for their own good—they certainly were not cowards. The tradition of the tough individual who fought the good fight and died the good death was still strong in the land in the 1830s.

One story, which some historians discount, is how the uneasy truce between Bowie and Travis was settled for good on February 21 by means of a serious accident. Helping to mount a cannon on one of the walls, Bowie fell fifteen feet, breaking some ribs and his hip. This injury, added to his mysterious ailment, took Bowie completely out of the action. He could now barely make it out of his bed.

Travis was in complete charge now, but even so, Bowie's mere presence was a boost to morale. In a journal that Davy Crockett kept during the siege are these words: "He is worth a dozen common men in a situation like ours. Colonel Bowie's illness continues, but he manages to crawl from his bed every day that his comrades may see him. His presence alone is a tower of strength."[1]

On the evening of February 22, 1836, most of the residents of the Alamo gathered in town for a party to celebrate the birthday of America's first president, George Washington. It was a rip-roaring party, the second in as many nights, with dancing, drinking, and fiery oratory.

As they partied, Santa Anna's army was camped on the banks of the Medina River, only eighteen miles away. Inside the walls of the Alamo were just ten men. The party broke up around midnight, and everyone went home to sleep.

During the night, when some members of the nearby Mexican community heard the rumor that Santa Anna was near, they quickly left town—the racket caused by their sudden departure woke Travis. He asked them what was going on and was horrified at their answer.

Travis climbed to the top of the tower of the Church of San Fernando, the highest spot in town, and gazed out into the dawn to try to glimpse any sign of Santa Anna. He saw nothing, and climbed back down, leaving one soldier as lookout.

As soon as Travis returned to his quarters, the lookout cried that he had seen the dawn sunlight glinting off something—maybe the lanceheads of advancing cavalry? Travis climbed up again, but he could see nothing. Was it a case of nerves on the part of the lookout?

He sent two soldiers out to ride around and see firsthand. A mile and a half south of the Alamo they crested a hill to find themselves viewing hundreds of Mexican cavalry ready for battle. They spun around their horses and thundered back into the gates of the Alamo.

The church bell rang out a warning. The Mexicans in town quickly scattered, trying to get out of the

Travis looked for Santa Anna's army from the tower of the Church of San Fernando, the highest spot in the town.

coming cross fire and to avoid Santa Anna's wrath if he suspected that they had been sympathetic to the Texans. Travis's soldiers scurried onto the walls of the Alamo. Santa Anna later claimed that if he and his troops had taken a less leisurely breakfast that morning they could have taken the garrison completely by surprise and won without a fight.

At this point there were 146 soldiers in the Alamo ready to defend it with their lives. Could they expect hundreds of armed helpers any minute? No one knew. Earlier, Travis had sent out another message by mounted courier that ended, "For God's sake and the sake of our country, send us reinforcements." Would reinforcements arrive in time?

"No Quarter, No Mercy"

General Santa Anna rode into town with his personal staff around him. Twelve-year-old Enrique Esparza was present and recalled the scene: "I saw him dismount. He did not hitch his horse. He gave the bridle to a lackey. I will never forget the face or the figure of Santa Anna. He had a very broad face and high cheek bones. He had a hard and cruel look and his countenance was a very sinister one."[2] Later, the Esparza family joined the people in the Alamo, while Enrique's uncle Francisco was a soldier in Santa Anna's army.

The Texans, joined by Tejanos like Enrique Esparza and his family, looked out over the walls of the Alamo, the dust barely beginning to settle from the fleeing Mexicans and the arriving army. They saw a chilling sight.

Santa Anna had raised a huge bloodred banner from the tower of the Church of San Fernando. Its meaning was clear: "No quarter." Many battles in those days could end with little bloodshed when one side offered to surrender. The opposing officers would meet and negotiate. Often the losing side was allowed to march off, sometimes even with their weapons, if they agreed to stop fighting for the moment.

On that day, with this scarlet flag flapping in the cool breeze of the Texas morning, there would be no terms worked out between courteous disputants. If the defenders of the Alamo did give up, which was definitely not in their minds, their surrender would have to be total. And even under these conditions, surrender might not save their lives.

But even as Santa Anna had his army raise the red flag, he also had his bugler blow the signal for peace talks. In answer to this call, Travis fired the eighteen-pounder cannon, the largest gun in the Alamo. It was an act of bravura, an insult flung back at Santa Anna.

Although Bowie was now confined to bed with his illness and injuries, he was not beyond a bit of meddling. He sent out a man under a flag of truce to ask if Santa Anna had, indeed, offered to talk. The answer came back, swift and clear—no, no mercy, no negotiations. Then to make it clear to all that he and not Bowie was, in fact, in charge, Travis sent out a messenger of his own who got the same unyielding answer from Santa Anna.

After this disagreement, Bowie collapsed, totally worn out, and played little part in the battle. Travis was now in charge, and even under the circumstances, he must have breathed a sigh of relief. He still had to deal with Santa Anna, but at least Jim Bowie was out of his way.

At Travis's side still was Davy Crockett, whose only request was that he be allowed to serve as a "high private." In anything from a fist fight in a cantina to an attack from the Mexican Army, no soldier could ask for a better companion.

Sizing Up the Enemy

As Santa Anna's troops marched into the area and began to surround the Alamo, Travis whipped his army into a flurry of activity. He assigned guards to various sections of the walls, and got the cannon ready.

Travis realized how little food had been stockpiled inside the Alamo. Since only a small part of the Mexican Army had actually arrived, the defenders were able to sneak in and out. In fact, until the time of the final assault, it was possible, in the dark of night, for a person to steal in and out even on horseback. The series of eloquent pleas for help that Travis sent past the Mexican sentries bears testimony to this.

Santa Anna considered attacking right away, but he did not know how many soldiers were inside the Alamo. His greatest fear, however, was that hundreds of armed Texans would come thundering up behind his troops as they attacked. His dilemma was this: Should he attack now while his own army was not yet up to full strength in order to avoid the later arrival of enemy reinforcements? Or should he wait, let his own army arrive in force, and then attack?

So, while Travis sent out urgent messages for help, Santa Anna basically acted the same way, dispatching

SOURCE DOCUMENT

To the people of Texas & all Americans in the world—Fellow citizens & compatriots

I am besieged, by a thousand or more of the Mexicans under Santa Anna. . . . *I shall never surrender or retreat.* Then, I call on you in the name of Liberty, of patriotism, & everything dear to the American character, to come to our aid, with all dispatch—The enemy is receiving reinforcements daily & will no doubt increase to three or four thousand. . . . I am determined to sustain myself as long as possible & die like a soldier who never forgets what is due to his own honor & that of his country.

—VICTORY OR DEATH.
William Barret Travis.
Lt. Col. Comdt.[3]

William Travis sat down in his makeshift quarters and penned one of the most stirring patriotic messages—and one of the most desperate—in American history.

riders southward to urge the rest of his army to get there quickly. Most of his artillery and about five hundred soldiers were stuck in the mud a few miles out of town. Another large portion of his army was still several days march to the south.

Santa Anna ordered his troops to harass the defenders with constant, but not very effective, musket fire. He wanted to prevent the movement of people and supplies into or out of the Alamo. As Santa Anna supervised the placement of his artillery and cannon, he used the knowledge that in some places the walls were over two feet thick. So he placed his cannon to fire at the spots where they had some chance of smashing through.

The largest cannon in Santa Anna's army that had arrived in San Antonio were the eight-pounders, and he took a long and careful look at the outer perimeter of the Alamo to see where they might do the most damage. After only a few well-aimed shots, one of the small Mexican cannon knocked the biggest Texan cannon, the eighteen-pounder, off its mounting.

The gun was quickly repaired, but now the defenders knew that they were dealing with some skilled artillerymen. Slowly, even to the most optimistic or foolhardy defenders of the Alamo, the idea finally sank in that without reinforcements they would all die.

The Siege

A tiny settlement, La Villita, stood only a few dozen yards from the front gate of the Alamo. Two hundred

Mexicans hid behind the huts and then charged the walls. The continuing existence of these huts was another example of incomplete planning on the part of the Texans. Some historians believe that the defenders should have demolished them before the Mexicans arrived in order to deny the enemy the opportunities for protection, however meager, that they offered.

The Mexicans charged. Furious musket and cannon fire from inside the Alamo beat them back. That night, a raiding party of Texans, covered by gunfire from inside, burned down the huts.

Santa Anna did not know that the defenders had a working well inside the walls and another skirmish

The Texans fired their cannon at the Mexican Army as they charged the Alamo.

occurred when the Mexicans tried to dam an irrigation canal that brought water into the Alamo from the west.

The cold, black nights of that February were lit by the ring of campfires in the encircling Mexican camp. Santa Anna ordered his regimental bands to play. The defenders also used music to keep up morale. One night Davy Crockett with his famous fiddle and John McGregor with his Scottish bagpipes participated in a musical "duel" for the entertainment of the defenders.

For the Mexicans, who had probably never heard bagpipes before, the strange music from inside the Alamo must have seemed eerie indeed.

The Mexican blockade was never complete. During these days and nights of cannon shots and waiting, Travis sent out at least sixteen couriers, begging for reinforcements.[4]

One of these couriers was Juan Seguin, one of the Tejanos who fought alongside the Texans. Travis dispatched Seguin and an aide on horseback. It was the night of the fiery raid on the shantytown of La Villita outside the walls of the Alamo. The two men went undetected at first.

A little while later they encountered several Mexican cavalrymen at a road block some distance from the Alamo. Seguin rode on, speaking to them in his educated Spanish. The soldiers, apparently thinking that he was an officer come to give them more orders, did not fire.

Suddenly they saw, by the light of their campfire, who was approaching and sprang onto their horses. It was too late. Seguin knew the terrain and easily got away.

It was almost as easy to get into the Alamo as it was to get out. One night in the midst of the siege, about thirty-two reinforcements arrived on horseback. One of the Alamo's sentries fired a shot at them, hitting one of the men in the foot.

As other sentries cocked their muskets, the injured rider let loose with a long, loud, foul oath that immediately convinced the guards that these could only be Texans. No one else swore in such quantity or with such style. The men rode in and were, of course, very welcome. They knew that they were almost certainly volunteering to die beside the men and women already in the Alamo, and their courage and sacrifice has become legendary in Texan history.

According to some accounts, the new men brought the total number inside the walls to between 180 and 190. That was a small piece of good news. The bad news was that Santa Anna was receiving reinforcements too. That same day, over nine hundred Mexican soldiers arrived, some of them elite troops—well trained and experienced in battle. With them was a seven-inch howitzer, a cannon capable of lofting bombs over the walls.

Conditions Grow Worse

The situation inside the Alamo was grim. The walls had originally been built as protection against hostile

Native Americans. The steady assault of the Mexican cannon balls was much different than that of arrows. Ominous cracks showed up in the stone and adobe walls as Santa Anna's artillery, literally, chipped away at them.

Ammunition was running low. Travis, Crockett, Dickinson, and the others had fired as often as they could reload early in the siege. Now, with gunpowder running low, they knew that they had to make every shot count. Food ran low too—if all the Mexicans did was wait them out, their days were still numbered.

The stone and adobe walls of the Alamo began to crack upon being pummelled with cannonfire. The Long Barracks are a part of the Alamo that still stands today.

With each passing day, Santa Anna moved his artillery closer, making it more and more effective.

On the morning of March 3, another large group of Santa Anna's soldiers arrived. Santa Anna was exasperated at their delay. He had sent them orders to make haste, but their general had called a five-day halt so that they could rest. There were now twenty-five hundred Mexican soldiers surrounding the Alamo.

By now it was very clear to Santa Anna and his generals that conditions inside the Alamo were desperate. Oddly, none of the generals suggested waiting for the defenders to run out of food—a simple strategy that could have easily succeeded with little or no bloodshed. Some of his senior officers did suggest showing mercy to the Texans, since they were so clearly no longer a real threat.

Santa Anna heard them out, but said, "Against the daring foreigners opposing us, the honor of our Nation and our Army is at stake."[5] The army, he ordered, would rest and prepare on March 4 and 5, and be ready to storm the walls on the morning of March 6, 1836. The Mexican leader left nothing to chance. He carefully prepared his plan of attack.

Santa Anna's Battle Plans

General Cos, who had suffered such a stinging defeat in this very town in December 1835, would lead four hundred soldiers to attack the northwest corner of the Alamo. He had, of course, promised not to fight again against the Texans as a condition of his release

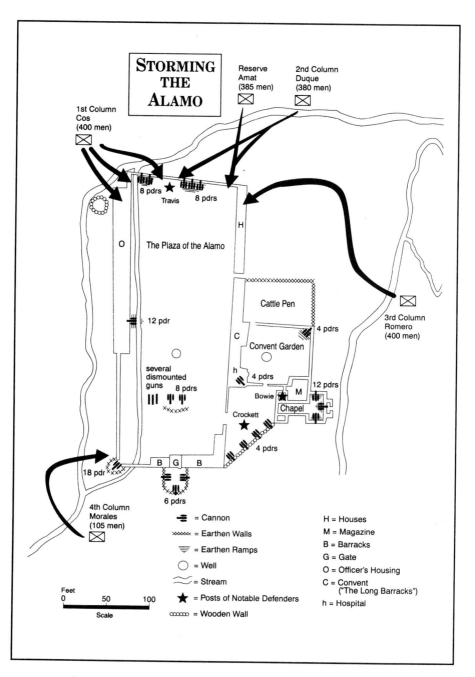

Santa Anna's battle plans for the storming of the Alamo.

after he lost the Alamo to them the previous December. Now he broke his promise, or perhaps, considered that a promise forced out of him was no promise at all.

Cos would lead his troop into the fury of five eight-pounders and musket fire at the northwest corner. Travis was positioned at the center of the northern wall. For Cos it would be a chance to redeem himself in Santa Anna's eyes and regain his personal pride.

Colonel Duque would also lead his troop, 380 in number, against that northern wall, aiming at a weak spot. Four hundred seasoned soldiers under the leadership of Colonel Romero would attack the eastern wall. One hundred crack infantry fighters under Colonel Morales would try to take the south wall. This attack by Morales with only one hundred soldiers was probably meant as a diversion.

Part of Santa Anna's precise plan was to name exactly which officers were to take over in case the officer leading an attack was killed or wounded. He himself would rush in to take Cos's place if necessary.

The reserve troops, to be called into action wherever they were needed at the moment, numbered 385 of the best troops. The cavalry, 350 men under Brigadier General Ramirez y Sesma, were assigned to watch the surrounding area for anyone trying to flee. The calvary's other job was to be sure that no last-minute reinforcements galloped unopposed to the aid of the people in the Alamo.

Santa Anna made two other decisions that made the attack more effective. He knew that he had about four hundred soldiers in his army who had very little training and no experience in combat. They were to remain in camp. He also ordered that his own artillery was to remain silent during the attack so that so-called "friendly fire"—artillery fire from his cannon—would not endanger his army.

The night before the attack, Santa Anna ordered that an earthwork (hole) be dug as close as possible to the north wall of the Alamo so that his troops could attack from there instead of charging across such a long stretch of open field. It was a sound idea, but the preparations kept some of the Mexican Army awake for most of the night. All in all, according to military analysts, it was an excellent plan of attack.[6]

The night of March 5 was a sleepless night for the Mexican soldiers as they prepared for the attack. It was a night without much rest for the defenders of the Alamo, too.

On March 4, Santa Anna's army had moved several cannon as close as possible to the northwest corner and had begun to pound away at the wall with cannonball after cannonball.

"VICTORY OR DEATH"

Men with shovels, buckets, and even handfuls of earth did what they could to pile a big mound of earth behind the wall. The last of the ammunition was passed out, and extra muskets were given to the soldiers on watch.

One of the last known letters carried out of the Alamo on March 3 was short and to the point. It ended with the words, "God and Texas! Victory or Death!"

Just after dark on March 5, Travis dispatched one last courier—James L. Allen, who was one of the youngest men in the Alamo. There were others who were perhaps better riders, but Travis may have felt that the young Allen deserved the chance to live a few more years.

At this point, Travis may have made one last try to negotiate with Santa Anna. Victory—even survival—was impossible if there was a fight, and the defenders had already achieved their military purpose, to delay the Mexican Army while Sam Houston and others got ready to fight. Even though Texans had been sneaking in and out during the siege, for all of the Texans to escape was virtually impossible. They were tired, hungry, and escape routes were now patrolled by Santa Anna's cavalry. Travis must have believed—or at least hoped—that Santa Anna's red flag signalling "no quarter" had been boasting rather than his true intention.

Santa Anna would not even discuss the matter, saying there could be "no guarantees for traitors." He considered them traitors, of course, because they were mostly Mexican citizens fighting against the Mexican Army. The ones who were not nominal Mexican citizens were trespassers in Mexico.

It was at this point that one of the most famous events of the story of the Alamo happened—or did not happen. Even though for generations Texas schoolchildren grew up being told the story, historians are doubtful.

A Line in the Sand

On the last day on which there would be any hope of escaping, the story tells, Travis gathered all the Texans together and gave them a stirring speech. Then, with his sword, he drew a line in the sand and invited any man who was willing to stay and fight alongside him to cross the line. Any man who did not choose to fight would be allowed to leave—it might still be possible to sneak out under cover of darkness.

At first, the men crossed in small groups. Jim Bowie, by this time very ill, urged his friends to carry his bed across. Only one man, Louis Rose, did not cross. First, they say, he fainted dead away. When he came to he still refused to cross. Travis, true to his word, gave Rose some food and water and boosted him over the wall. Louis Rose, or a man who claimed to be him, later told this tale.

So after Travis either did or did not draw his line in the sand, it had come to this: an unusually warm night on March 5, with the Mexican Army preparing to attack with overwhelming force and no mercy, and an almost full moon to light everyone's last-minute military preparations and thoughts of their own mortality.

Travis, accompanied by Joe, his twenty-three-year-old African-American slave, moved about the eerily lit compound, talking to his troops, inspecting guard posts, giving what cheer and encouragement he could. He gave a gift to Angelina, the small daughter of Captain Almeron and Susanna Dickinson. He threaded his gold ring with a cat's eye stone through a piece of ribbon and hung it around the girl's neck.[1] Rarely have soldiers prepared for battle more certain of defeat and death, and more determined to die with honor and glory.

Dawn Breaks

Saturday, March 5, 1836, at midnight, the Mexican cavalry were the first to stir. With the ordinary foot soldiers digging a preparatory ditch, the cavalry was given a special job to do.

They fed, watered, and saddled their mounts, and then rode into the surrounding countryside. Their assignment was to catch and kill anyone trying to escape the Alamo, and to fight off any last-minute help from outside.

Before long the infantry began to get ready, the officers checked their equipment and marched it silently into position. Even as Travis went to bed, most of the Mexican Army was in place and ready, waiting only for first light.

All this was done by the Mexicans quietly and with great skill. None of the men who Travis had posted outside between the walls of the Alamo and the Mexicans saw or heard anything.

Just minutes after 5:00 A.M., as faint light began to streak the eastern sky, the battle commenced when soldiers in one of the northern columns started yelling "Viva Santa Anna." Santa Anna turned to his bugler José María Gonzalez and ordered him to sound the *Adelante!* (Forward!), which was immediately taken up by all the buglers of the Mexican Army. This must have been a terrible sound to the defenders inside the walls of the Alamo.

The Battle at the Alamo

With drawn swords, the Mexican officers screamed, *"Arriba!"* ("Attack!") The four attacking columns raced forward across the two hundred to three hundred yards toward the Alamo walls.

Captain John Baugh, who had just come on duty as officer of the day, heard the trumpets and shouted "The Mexicans are coming!" The guards on the walls began to fire at the onrushing and totally exposed Mexican soldiers. They began to fall, but still they came.

Sleepy Alamo defenders climbed out of their bedrolls and rushed to their positions on the walls. More musket fire tore into the advancing Mexicans. Baugh's cry and the firing woke Travis, who buckled on his sword and hurried to the wall, followed by his African-American slave Joe.

The Mexicans, under order to hold their fire until given the command, ran forward. But as soon as

Dawn at the Alamo *by H.A. McArdle shows the famous battle.*

someone cried out, "¡Viva Santa Anna!" and "¡Viva La Republica!" they began to rush forward, firing their muskets—without leaving time to reload.

Travis reached the top of the north wall just as the Mexicans were putting their scaling ladders into position. He fired his shotgun into the crowd of soldiers below. Joe fired down at them too, then turned to see Travis falling away from the wall—he had been shot through the forehead.

William Barret Travis, the courageous young officer who uttered the famous cry "Victory or Death!," is believed to be one of the first Texans to die at the Alamo.

The fighting was fierce. The Texans fired their cannon, loaded with deadly doses of scrap iron. Many of the defenders had three or four loaded muskets at hand, and they fired down on the attackers.

The first of the ladders collapsed under the weight of the men—they had been hastily constructed and were too flimsy to hold more than one or two. The Mexicans could not make it up the wall, but to run back across the open ground was hopeless, too. Men began to bunch up in the relative safety just below the walls.

Some of the Mexicans fell back in confusion, and for a moment it looked as though the attack had failed. But almost at once the officers rushed in, swearing and cursing, urging the soldiers to attack again. Amid "Vivas!" for Santa Anna and Mexico, the attackers charged again.

The Mexican soldiers, charging the high walls and lethal musket and cannon fire, were fierce and brave. But brave as they were, the high walls and defending gunfire kept them from their goal. Again, they tried to crowd together below the walls, each soldier seeking out safety. Soldiers inside and outside the walls were reloading and catching their breath, the battle at a momentary lull.

Santa Anna sprang into action. He ordered the reserves to attack the northwestern corner of the wall, with the brilliantly uniformed and plumed members of his personal staff to inspire them. To his bugler Gonzalez, he gave the order to sound the advance. Every bugle in the Mexican Army echoed the call. Colonel de la Pena later wrote that this decisive moment "inspired us to scorn life and to embrace death."[2]

More ladders were brought into position. Some Mexicans discovered that in places where the walls had recently been repaired they could simply scamper up using rough spots as hand- and foot-holds.

The hastily reloading Texans were simply no match for the musket fire from hundreds of Mexican soldiers. Texans fell wounded or dead from the walls as more and more Mexicans attacked. Some Mexican soldiers got up on top of the northern wall. Jumping down into the plaza of the Alamo, they found a small gate and opened it, letting in more attackers. In minutes, the entire northern wall was in Mexican hands, and soldiers poured into the plaza.

Captain Dickinson was on top of the church at the other end of the plaza. For just a moment, Dickinson left his post to run to his family to say good-bye. He held his wife Susanna and his daughter Angelina in his arms for the last time. "Great God, Sue," he cried. "The Mexicans are inside our walls! All is lost! If they spare you, love our child."[3] Then he ran back to his cannon to die firing.

The scrap iron blasts that his guns rained down on the attackers who were now inside the walls held them up—but only for a moment. At the same time, other Mexican soldiers took the big eighteen-pounder at bayonet-point and turned it around to fire at the defenders.

Mexican troops now poured in from three separate points on the walls. The Texans managed to hold back the Mexican soldiers for around forty-five minutes, then they retreated back into the convento, or Long Barracks, as Travis had ordered. Now would begin the most ferocious and personal part of the battle. With no time to reload their muskets, the fighters on both sides would be face to face with only the length of a bayoneted musket or a swinging saber between them. Now the men killing each other could see clearly into each other's eyes.

The first fall-back positions were the trenches that Travis had ordered dug in the hard soil of the plaza. The trenches provided protection for a few minutes only. From there the defenders rushed to the momentary security of the many buildings around the edges of the big plaza.

Holes had been knocked in the inside walls so that the defenders could retreat from one to the other, fighting hand-to-hand as they went. The Texans made their last stand, fighting in small groups or alone, dying proudly in the battle against the ferocious invaders.

Some tried to surrender—all were slain. At about 6:00 A.M., roughly an hour into the battle, the Mexican flag of red, white, and green with the fierce eagle holding a snake in its beak and perched on a cactus was raised in triumph over the Alamo. The firing tapered off as the last of the defenders were taken from hiding places and killed. Bowie, ill and unable to leave his bed, was shot and bayoneted where he lay.

In the aftermath of the Battle of the Alamo, all of its defenders lay dead.

Several men who were taken alive were not so lucky. Of the few Mexicans from the area who had taken refuge in the Alamo, one boy and an old man were taken to Santa Anna. One of his officers suggested that perhaps mercy was in order. The general's order stood: "No mercy!"

According to Colonel de la Pena, an eyewitness, this is how the defenseless men were dealt with:

> Several officers who were with the President, who perhaps had not been present at the point of the danger . . . pushed forward, in order to impress their general, and, with swords in hand, fell upon these miserable, defenseless men . . . [who] died without complaining and without humiliating themselves.[4]

Silence fell upon the Alamo. All of its defenders and many of its attackers lay dead.

It is a strange quirk of history that the Texans who fought and now lay dead at the Alamo played a very important part in helping gain independence for Texas—but they were not to know it.

THE AFTERMATH

There had been plenty of talk about independence from Mexico, about making Texas an independent country, but talk is all it was. The Texans had chosen leaders, men who had almost no real authority because there was not yet a genuine country to rule. Many of the defenders of the Alamo believed in independence for Texas. Others still had some faith that they could go on living as citizens of Mexico. These people fought against Santa Anna's usurped totalitarian powers and for renewed life for the Mexican Constitution of 1824.

In fact, one of the flags that flew over the Alamo was the Mexican tricolor with 1824 in the center, symbolizing loyalty to that Constitution.

Declaration of Texan Independence
Until March 1, 1836, after Santa Anna's army fired their cannon at the walls of the Alamo, there was no Republic of Texas. On that day, in a tiny village on the banks of the Brazos River, grandly called

Washington-on-the-Brazos, delegates from American and Mexican settlements met. They arrived in wagons and on horseback, maneuvering around the stumps that still stood in the dirt road outside a ramshackle building.

While the fighting was going on at the Alamo, they met in an unfinished building. The building had cloth instead of glass in the windows, and was owned by a gunsmith and part-time preacher named Noah Ayres.

If the setting was humble, the oratory was far from it. These men met with the expressed purpose of setting up a government completely independent from Mexico—or from any other country. After a day of patriotic speeches they did just that, with a declaration of independence that was very similar to the one that the Americans of their grandfathers' generation used to cut their ties with England in 1776.

After much arguing and patriotic outbursts, Sam Houston was elected "Commander-in-Chief of all the land forces of the Texan army, both regulars, volunteers and militia . . . and endowed with all the rights, privileges and powers due to a Commander-in-Chief in the United States of America."

The good news was that Sam Houston was in charge of the army—the bad news was that there was not much of an army to command. There were only men without uniforms carrying their own weapons. The lucky ones had horses.

The delegates stayed around the small town to draft a new constitution and to elect a government.

They stayed until March 18. On March 6, a plea for reinforcements had arrived from Travis. The Alamo, it said, was being heavily bombarded—the end was near. The delegates did not know it, of course, but by this time the Alamo had fallen, and Travis and the others were dead.

The Brave Heroes

As closely as historians can estimate, between 180 and 252 people died in the defense of the Alamo. They were a mixed lot. Among the dead were three brothers from Tennessee—James, George, and Edward Taylor. The youngest to die was probably

This monument is a tribute to the brave defenders of the Alamo.

Galba Fuqua, sixteen; the oldest was Gordon C. Jennings, fifty-seven.

No one will ever know for sure, but they seem to have come from at least twenty-eight different states and countries. The largest number, at least thirty-four, were from Davy Crockett's state of Tennessee, with Virginia (thirteen) and Kentucky (twelve) close behind. But there were also twelve men from Ireland, twelve from England, one from Denmark, four from Scotland, and one from Wales. Nine Tejanos died also. Twenty-three are listed simply as "unknown."[1]

About seventy Mexican soldiers died in taking the Alamo, and approximately three hundred were seriously wounded. Because Santa Anna had no doctors with him, most of the wounded died from infection, exposure, loss of blood, and shock over the next few days. Since Santa Anna could probably have taken the Alamo with little or no bloodshed if he had waited a few days, it can be argued that these men died not for the glory of Mexico but for the glory of their general. "What are the lives of soldiers," Santa Anna said after the battle, "more than so many chickens?"[2]

One African-American slave, a man named John who was owned by Francis de Sauque, died in the attack. Because he assumed that they had not fought willingly, Santa Anna spared the other African Americans—Travis's slave Joe and Bowie's freedman Sam.

Over the years it has been rumored that two or three other defenders survived, but nobody knows for sure. One Mexican Army deserter who fought along with the defenders is said to have locked himself in the Alamo's one jail cell just before the Mexican soldiers stormed in. He claimed he had been captured and held against his will.

One interesting footnote to history is the great difference in how many men on each side supposedly died, based on the testimony of various witnesses. The tendency of American historians is to inflate the number of Mexican attackers and casualties, and downplay the number of Alamo defenders. A couple of Mexican extremes: Santa Anna claimed that his men had killed 606 defenders, whereas the most accurate number seems to have been between 180 and 252.

A number of women and children were inside the Alamo and were allowed by Santa Anna to live. Bowie's sisters-in-law, Juana Alsbury and Gertrudis Navarro, survived the attack, as did Trinidad Saucedo, Dona Petra, and a few others. Several children also survived.

But it is Susanna Dickinson, wife of artillery Captain Almeron Dickinson, and their daughter Angelina, about fifteen months old, who carried the story back to Sam Houston and the newly formed Texan army.

The Woman on Horseback

Right after the sound of gunshots ceased, the Mexicans herded the women and children into a corner of the church. Susanna Dickinson, almost certain now that her husband was dead along with the others, crouched against the stone wall holding Angelina tightly in her arms.

A guard spoke. "Is Mrs. Dickinson here?" he asked. "Is Mrs. Dickinson here? If you value your life speak up."[3] Susanna rose and faced General Manuel Castrillon. As she was being marched from the church she heard a gunshot and felt a stab of pain in her right calf. Whether she was shot accidentally or in anger she never found out, but the wound was minor.

As she stepped over pools of blood and past bodies, she claimed to recognize the crumpled form of Davy Crockett, his bloody coonskin cap on the ground nearby.

She was taken, with Angelina, into the temporary quarters of General Santa Anna himself. Santa Anna took an immediate liking to the beautiful little Angelina, and she to him. He pleaded with Susanna to let him take them both to Mexico City, and to let him raise Angelina as his own child. The little girl would have the best of everything Santa Anna promised, and Susanna's lot in life would be excellent.

Susanna's state of mind can only be imagined: As far as she was concerned her friends and her own husband had just been murdered by this man. She was in no mood to trust him or hand over her only child. She told him "no."

If she could not recognize a wonderful opportunity, Santa Anna told her, he would turn her loose to suffer the fate of the rest of the Texas renegades whom he would soon be tracking down and killing. He called for an African-American servant named Ben, and told him to accompany the woman and child across the empty stretches of Texas to deliver a message to the chief renegade himself—Sam Houston.

We have only Susanna Dickinson's word for the story of the attempted adoption, but it does go along with other attempts on the part of the eccentric general to adopt American children. What we do know

---

SOURCE DOCUMENT

The General-in-Chief of the Army of Operations of the Mexican Republic, to the inhabitants of Texas:

Citizens! . . . a parcel of audacious adventurers, maliciously protected by some inhabitants of a neighboring republic dared to invade our territory . . .

It became necessary to check and chastise such enormous daring; and in consequence, some exemplary punishments have already taken place. . . .

If we are bound to punish the criminal, we are not less compelled to protect the innocent. . . .

Return to your homes and dedicate yourselves to domestic duties. . . . The Supreme Government has taken you under its protection and will seek for your good.[4]

General Santa Anna sent a letter, dated March 7, 1836, to the Americans, warning them away from Texas.

for sure is that Santa Anna put Susanna and Angelina on a horse, gave them water and food, and pointed them toward the town of Gonzalez, over seventy miles away. Was it gallantry that prevented him from killing her outright or just the desire to spread panic by the message he gave her? He sent her off with a warning for the rest of the Americans in Texas.

Carrying Santa Anna's message, Susanna Dickinson rode out of the Alamo. She rode past the appalling sight of the bodies of the defenders, many of them her friends, one of them her husband and the father of her tiny daughter, laid out on a huge stack of wood and put to the torch. Most received no rites, no burial; their bones turned to ash and dust to become part of the soil of the Alamo. In February of the following year, Captain Juan Seguin, who had left the Alamo during the siege as a courier, returned with the Texas army. He gathered what remains and ashes were left and buried them nearby. The spot where he did this is now lost to history.

Sam Houston arrived in the town of Gonzalez and received word from Mexicans who had fled that the Alamo had fallen. He sent out two scouts, Henry Karnes and the famous tracker Erastus "Deaf" Smith.

The ride from the Alamo toward Gonzalez was perilous and long for Susanna Dickinson. She had been pointed in the right direction, placed on a rough cattle trail, and told to ride until she came to the first lighted house. Comanches still roamed these hills, and perhaps wretched deserters from the Mexican Army or wandering thieves.

But Susanna Dickinson was a hardy woman and she rode until she was found by settlers and taken to Gonzalez. Her tale of what had happened to the defenders of the Alamo struck terror into the hearts of everyone. "For four and twenty hours," as R. E. Handy described the scene, "after the news reached us not a sound was heard save the wild shrieks of women and heartrending screams of their fatherless children."[5]

News spread quickly—in spite of his soothing words, Santa Anna was scouring Texas with murder in his heart. The citizens of Gonzalez stampeded, not as much because of Susanna Dickinson's news about the Alamo, but because of the rumor that Santa Anna was right behind her with two thousand troops.

Saddles were thrown on horses; a few prized possessions were tossed into wagons and men, women, and children left in panic, thus beginning the great escape that came to be known in Texas history as the Runaway Scrape.

Houston's Retreat

The defenses of Texas were in bad shape. With only about eleven hundred to thirteen hundred men in Sam Houston's new army, the troops would have been no match for Santa Anna if he had acted immediately. But Texas is a big place, and the Texan army was scattered: about 500 at Goliad under James W. Fannin, another 275 at Gonzalez, perhaps 200 at

Matagorda, and another 300 to 400 scattered all over the place.

To track them down would have been a huge job for Santa Anna, and it was a job that he could not start right away.

He still had only about half his army with him at the Alamo. His soldiers were exhausted from the siege and attack, and many were wounded. The wounded had to be given some sort of care, even if their prospects were not good. As the rest of the army rested, the cavalry was sent to scour the countryside for the enemy and forage for supplies.

Santa Anna was not worried about the Texas army. He had beaten them at the Alamo, and as soon as he caught up with the rest of this ragged bunch of fighting Texans, he would kill them too. He was supremely confident.

Technically, the headquarters of the Texas army was in Gonzalez, the small town that Susanna Dickinson rode to with her tale of horror and death. Sam Houston was there and he ordered a strategic retreat. His army—badly fed, ill-equipped, with little ammunition, and almost no training—was no match for Santa Anna's well-armed and disciplined troops, and Houston knew it.

His strategy was to retreat and stay out of Santa Anna's way while he whipped these soldiers into shape as a fighting force. Along the way he could gather more horses and more supplies. A few of the more hotheaded men in his command wanted to ride straight at Santa Anna's army and have it out then and there. Houston won out, convincing his men of the wisdom of his strategy.

The Palm Sunday Massacre

Fannin, meanwhile, was still sitting on his good intentions in Goliad. Well-meaning, maybe, Fannin was basically incapable of dealing with crises. He was the man who had earlier turned back in his attempt to go to the Alamo because of a couple of broken wagons. Now, when he received Houston's orders to evacuate, he took the time to try to persuade the settlers in the area to leave. If he had simply saddled up and ridden out with his troops, the settlers would have surely followed in great haste.

But Fannin hesitated. Mexican General José Urrea, a highly professional fighting officer, was on his way with five hundred soldiers. Goliad had a good fort, a much easier place to defend than the Alamo. If Fannin had stood and fought, he could have pinned down Urrea for weeks, and forced Santa Anna to bring his army as reinforcements.

Retreat? "Yes," Fannin said, and ordered his soldiers to bury the big cannon so that the Mexicans could not get them, wasting more time. Then he changed his mind, and had the cannon dug up again. Meanwhile fate, in the form of General Urrea, was thundering down on the unfortunate West Point dropout.

The list of mistakes that Fannin made makes a dismal story. When he finally did retreat, he did it badly. Little food or water was taken for the people or the animals that pulled the wagons. With the Mexicans in hot pursuit, Fannin ordered his column to halt about a mile from Coleto Creek.

His officers pointed out that that single mile could mean that they would have ample water and some cover from the trees along the creek. But Fannin insisted on his way, and his little army took up a position in a slight hollow in the middle of a large open area, with no natural cover and no water.

With the Mexicans now shooting at them, Fannin decided to try to make it to the creek. His soldiers were again pinned down halfway there. Fannin surrendered, and 442 men were taken prisoner.

A few days later, Santa Anna ordered them all executed as "pirates." Many of the Mexican soldiers were horrified, but they could not go against the orders of the powerful man. Some did manage to spare the lives of the doctors of the group, and some others were spared by individual Mexican officers who were brave enough to go against Santa Anna.

But the fate of 342 Texans was not so lucky. Fannin and the other prisoners were taken to Goliad and on Palm Sunday in 1836, they were taken to an open area and shot. When word of this massacre reached Sam Houston and his army, anger again fired their resolve. They wanted to fight, but Houston knew that they were not ready yet.

Training a Growing Army

With Santa Anna scouring the land for them, Houston moved his army skillfully, living off the land, training his men as they retreated. He sent out "Deaf" Smith and other fine scouts to keep him advised of where Santa Anna was. Houston was always just out of reach of the bloodthirsty Mexican general.

Panicked groups of uprooted settlers headed for the relative safety of east Texas. Some of them just kept going, turning their wagons east and not looking back. They had had enough. Fairfax Gray, a wealthy

This political cartoon shows Santa Anna (center) and Cos (right) surrendering to Sam Houston (left). This reflects the anti-Mexican sentiment of many Americans after the defeat of the Alamo and Goliad.

Virginian in Texas, wrote, "thousands are moving off to the east. A constant stream of women and children, and some men, with wagons, carts and pack mules, are rushing across the Brazos night and day."[6]

Houston's wandering army lost some men to the exodus, but it slowly grew, mostly with new arrivals from the United States, men who wanted adventure and land. He drilled his new recruits, turning them into a fighting force, while keeping one step ahead of General Santa Anna. A gift arrived from the City of Cincinnati, the "Twin Sisters," two six-pound cannon.

Houston's task was not an easy one, but he was a man with a strong personality and was a born leader. Most of the men who joined him did not want to go to the trouble to train and drill and become regular soldiers, they just wanted some adventure. They wanted to fight. And they wanted to fight right now—anger boiled in them because of the men who died at the Alamo and at Goliad.

Santa Anna's troops, split up now under the leadership of various subordinates, fanned out and headed northeast on a search-and-destroy mission. Houston's army was their primary prey.

The mood in the part of the army that Santa Anna led personally was supremely confident. They had developed a taste for catching and killing these Texan "pirates," and they wanted more. They would soon have their chance.

On April 19, 1836, Sam Houston and his army decided to stop running. His small army, still not perfectly trained or armed, was spoiling for a fight. But Houston knew that soldiers who were hot to start a fight might not be as hot to

THE SWORD OF SAN JACINTO

continue fighting against the skill and experience of Santa Anna's army.

Win or Die

Houston, a wily and intelligent leader, chose the perfect spot to have it out. He deliberately let himself run out of territory. Houston chose a spot where his soldiers would have their backs to Buffalo Bayou and the San Jacinto River. Lynch's Ferry, although nearby, was not capable of handling a quick retreat.

Houston realized that unless he soon led his army into battle, they might revolt against his leadership and go off to fight Santa Anna on their own. As it was, without the immediate prospects of a good scrap, soldiers were riding off daily in small groups to help their families escape the wrath of the Mexican Army. So Sam Houston let himself be "trapped."

Win or die, that was the choice Houston gave his troop as they faced the camp of Santa Anna. The Mexicans could retreat if they needed to, but Houston's group could not. The words of Travis at the Alamo must have echoed in their minds: "Victory or Death!"

That evening, the night of April 21, was spent waiting and preparing. The Texans were hotblooded and anxious to avenge the Alamo and Goliad, the Mexicans supremely confident that the foe before them was puny. Houston kept busy before the battle reading by candlelight in his tent from Swift's *Gulliver's Travels* and Julius Caesar's *Gallic Wars*.[1]

When the sun rose, the Texans were up and ready to fight, and Houston might well have attacked then, but he held them back. He knew from captured dispatches that General Cos was on his way to reinforce Santa Anna. He decided he would rather attack after Cos got there than have Cos arrive in the middle of a battle. Better attack an enemy who is all in front of him.

Exact figures for the two armies that faced each other on the plain of San Jacinto that day are not available. A good estimate for the Texan force seems to be 918; for the Mexicans, after Cos arrived, it was approximately 1,200.[2]

So anxious was the Texan army to attack, and so fearful that they might even be ordered to retreat before Santa Anna, that Houston began to hear murmurs that he should be replaced with someone less careful and more hotblooded.

But Houston, as it turned out, knew exactly what he was doing. He sent six soldiers out to destroy a small bridge a few miles down river so that there would be absolutely no way to retreat. An interesting historical parallel is that in 1519, the Spaniard Cortés, attempting to take Mexico from the Aztecs, burned the ships on which he and his group had arrived. Cortés had given his army the same choice that Houston gave—fight or die, with no chance of retreat.

Minute by minute during that long day the suspense built—when would Houston lead them to the revenge that they hungered for? When? Houston knew exactly when. Not only was he a clever strategist, he was a smart psychologist too. He read the mood of Santa Anna and the Mexicans perfectly. When? Why, of course, during the middle of *siesta*, the traditional middle-of-the-afternoon snooze that is part of Mexican culture.

So little did Santa Anna and his officers rate the threat from Houston that most of them were asleep by 3:00 in the afternoon. Standard procedure for an army encamped in an open place, such as the plain of San Jacinto, is to place guards, called pickets, at some distance in front to give warning.

Incredibly, Santa Anna had no scouts watching the Texan camp from a distance. Nor were there any pickets. There were no guards at all—just dozing men, with only a few soldiers awake, doing laundry or chatting sleepily. Santa Anna was sleeping under a tree.

"Remember the Alamo"

Now, Houston told his army with a smile. Now was the time to attack. In a thin line stretching roughly from east to west across the field, Houston placed his soldiers, ready to advance. At 3:30 P.M.—astride Saracen, his beautiful white stallion, sword in hand—he motioned his troop forward.

The men stepped forward. The army's band, a black drummer and a German fifer, was ready to strike up a bawdy tune, the only song that they both knew. All this activity went completely unnoticed by the Mexicans. At about 4:30 P.M., the Texans emerged from some trees, and were finally spotted by a lone bugler. He sounded the alert.

Sleepy Mexican soldiers did their best to get organized, their officers running about issuing contradictory orders. The cavalry rushed to throw saddles on their horses, and artillerymen hurried to their cannon. Their efforts were too late.

Mexican soldiers of that time were not trained to fight as individuals, taking initiative on their own. Surprised as they were, unable to form into lines and columns so that their officers could tell them what to do, they were doomed.

Houston and his army rushed forward, firing cannon nicknamed the "Twin Sisters," one at each end of the long line of troops, and rushing forward. Saracen was hit, shot out from under Houston. He climbed on another horse and continued to lead the attack. Just a few minutes later Houston's second horse was shot out from under him, but this time the bullet also shattering the bones in Houston's foot.

The Mexicans tried to rally, but could not. They broke ranks and ran toward the rear. Then the cry rose from the throats of the Texans, a cry that would reverberate down through Texan and American history: "Remember the Alamo! Remember Goliad!" Hundreds of Mexicans, some of them crying out "Me no Alamo!" were killed. The actual fight lasted about eighteen minutes—the slaughter took longer.[3]

Sam Houston led his army to fight the Battle of San Jacinto in an effort to avenge the American deaths at the Alamo and Goliad.

Houston tried to stop the carnage, crying "Gentlemen, I applaud your bravery, but damn your manners!"[4] If the battle of the Alamo was a lopsided victory, with Mexicans slaughtering Texans, this battle was even worse.

Around nightfall, Houston sat under a tree with a doctor attending to his shattered foot. His officers brought him reports of how the day had gone.

SOURCE DOCUMENT

Towards sunset, a woman on the outskirts of the camp began to clap her hands and shout "Hallelujah! Hallelujah!" Those about her thought her mad, but following her wild gestures, they saw one of the Hardings, of Liberty, riding for life towards the camp, his horse covered with foam, and he was waving his hat and shouting "San Jacinto! San Jacinto! The Mexicans are whipped and Santa Anna a prisoner!" The scene that followed beggars description. People embraced, laughed and wept and prayed, all in one breath. As the moon rose over the vast, flower-decked prairie, the soft southern wind carried peace to tired hearts and grateful slumber.[5]

Mrs. Terrell was one of the Texan settlers who was running for her life before the army of Santa Anna. Trapped against Buffalo Bayou, near the battlefield, she later wrote an account of the event.

Houston was told that about six hundred fifty Mexicans perished at San Jacinto. After events calmed down a bit, over seven hundred were taken prisoner. Only about eighty escaped. These numbers, when added up, exceeded the total number of the Mexican Army, but the general picture was clear. It was one of the most one-sided battles in military history.

Amazingly, the Texan loss was tiny: two killed outright, with six more mortally wounded. Another eighteen were less seriously hurt, Sam Houston among them.

The Texans captured all the Mexican equipment—six hundred muskets, a six-pound cannon, two hundred pistols, and a considerable amount in gold. Some of the gold mysteriously disappeared before making it into the official Texas army strongboxes.

The Capture of Santa Anna

Another disappearance was General Santa Anna himself. The next day, the Texas cavalry searched the surrounding area for prisoners and brought back a disheveled man who was wearing a private's uniform. As soon as the man was put with the other prisoners, the prisoners leapt to attention and saluted their general and president.

Santa Anna was then brought to Houston, who lay under a tree. American soldiers cried out to lynch Santa Anna, but Houston said no. Hanging the president of Mexico would do them no good. If they could get him to sign a document recognizing Texan independence, it could insure their success.

Santa Anna seemed glad to do it. As he saw it, his recognition of the independence of the new Republic and his written orders to all his troops to leave Texas were actually invalid because the documents were written and signed while he was in enemy hands.

Asked what he wanted done with the hundreds of Mexican corpses on the battlefield of San Jacinto, he replied that he did not care. Asked later to give the reasons for his defeat, he accepted no personal responsibility, saying, "Fortune had turned her back on me."[6]

Major General Vicente Filisola was now in command of the Mexican forces in Texas. Filisola and other officers were so used to obeying Santa Anna that they took the order to leave at face value. Four thousand undefeated Mexican soldiers were soon marching south. Texas was an independent republic.

As a new country, Texas could not very well hold prisoner the president of their neighbor to the south. As soon as Santa Anna was released and back in Mexico, he disavowed the agreements that he had signed and promised to take back Texas. Yet Mexico's own situation was so chaotic for the next ten years that Santa Anna's threat was a hollow one.

In July 1836, Texans chose a president and a vice president—Sam Houston and Mirabeau Buonaparte Lamar—and voted 3,277 to 91 to seek annexation to the United States of America. In September 1836, with great emotion and to roaring applause, President Sam Houston unbuckled and handed over to the Texas House of

THE NEW NATION BECOMES THE "LONE STAR" STATE

Representatives the sword he had carried at San Jacinto.

No longer a man of war, he wanted now to be a man of peace, leading the respectable people of his new nation in the ways of reconciliation and tranquility. That was not to be, of course, with angry Mexicans to the south who did not recognize this new land of "pirates," and warring Comanches still riding out of the hills to attack the settlers.

The Republic of Texas was perhaps unique in history in being a new nation whose goal from the very beginning was to cease to exist. The republic

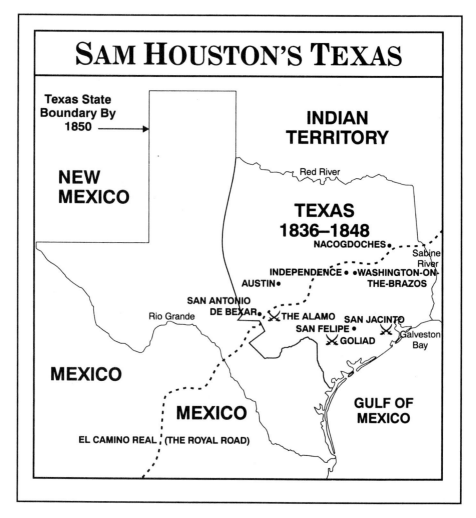

SAM HOUSTON'S TEXAS

Texas State
Boundary By
1850

NEW
MEXICO

INDIAN
TERRITORY

Red River

TEXAS
1836–1848

NACOGDOCHES

Sabine
River

INDEPENDENCE • •WASHINGTON-ON-
THE-BRAZOS

AUSTIN•

SAN ANTONIO
DE BEXAR• ✕THE ALAMO   SAN JACINTO
                   SAN FELIPE •   ✕
Rio Grande   ✕GOLIAD Galveston
                                          Bay

MEXICO

MEXICO

GULF OF
MEXICO

EL CAMINO REAL (THE ROYAL ROAD)

This map shows the expansion of Texas.

wanted to become part of the United States and would struggle for nine years to accomplish that goal.

The Republic of Texas

Unique in that way, the Republic of Texas was also very unusual in other ways. There was no money, no industry, no banks, no improved roads, and no organized schools. Only farmers, small-scale cattle ranchers, and more and more adventurers looking for cheap or free land peopled this new nation.

Annexation might have come much sooner if it had not been for the issue of slavery. John Quincy Adams denounced the Texas Revolution on the floor of the United States Congress. He said that the whole purpose of the war had been a plot for "the reestablishment of slavery in territory where it had already been abolished through Mexican law."[1]

During the ensuing years, the southern states wanted Texas admitted to the United States to bolster their position—the North wanted to prevent any such act. So the Republic of Texas continued to knock on the door, and forces in conflict within the United States barred the way.

In the tobacco and cotton growing states of the American South, slave owning was economically sound. In east Texas, a slave economy was beneficial for the landowners, but in the wide open spaces farther west, with small farms and cattle roaming vast ranges, it simply would not work as well.

What kept the Republic of Texas going in those early days was the hardiness of its people who lived off their land, with little day-to-day need for the rest of the world. The old-time settlers had experience fighting the Comanches and the newcomers learned quickly.

Even the threat of Mexico cooled considerably. The Mexican government was in collapse, the treasury was bankrupt, and the army was kept busy fighting off rival political factions.

As far as its own treasury was concerned, Texas was perhaps in worse shape than Mexico. Henry Smith, the Texas secretary of the Treasury could not perform his duties because he had no official stationery and no money to buy any![2]

Texas foreign policy was simple: Keep the war with Mexico down and the Native Americans quiet—and seek annexation to the United States.

In 1842, an old foe reappeared. Santa Anna invaded again, but with little energy and force. Before long he headed back to deal with the continuing economic and civil problems of his own country.

Also in 1842, the United States saw an even greater threat than the problems that a new slave state could cause: England began to show a real interest in Texas. The possibility of Texas allied with England and disputing control over the vast lands to the west was a threat that got Washington's immediate attention.

On December 29, 1845, President James Polk signed the act that made the Lone Star one of many stars in the flag of the United States. On February 19, 1846, the Texas flag was lowered, the new flag raised. The Republic of Texas was no more.

To this day, some Mexicans only half-jokingly refer to Texas, Arizona, New Mexico, and California as "the occupied territories to the north." They believe that this huge mass of land was taken from them unfairly and illegally by force of arms at a time when their country's government was at its weakest.

As soon as the news spread of Sam Houston's resounding victory at San Jacinto, new settlers began to pour into Texas. Sometimes whole communities from the United States picked up and headed for Texas. Some of the more restless rolled on west to California, but most made homes and farms in Texas.

Through the years of the republic and later when Texas was admitted to statehood, government policy was such that land was available. Native Americans and African Americans were not allowed to own land, but for white families who could not hope to own land elsewhere, Texas was wide open.

Another War with Mexico

When Texas was admitted to the United States in 1845, Mexico was horrified. Many there had felt that the Republic of Texas was just temporary and that sooner or later, preferably sooner, Texas would be theirs again. When their powerful neighbor to the north made Texas a state, anger boiled up.

The anger, and the conflict, became focused on the disputed territory between the Nueces River and the Río Grande (which continues to be called the Río Bravo by the Mexicans).

President James Polk sent Brigadier General Zachary Taylor into Texas to be ready for any hostilities. Taylor was a big man, with heavy features, half-closed eyes, and poor eyesight, who hated military pomp. He wore untidy and oddly assorted civilian clothes with only a single star on his cap to mark his rank. He rode a big, slow-moving white horse, sometimes with both legs slung casually over one side.

His mind seemed to move as slowly as his horse, but he was a reasonably competent military man, and his soldiers respected him. They called him "Old Rough and Ready."

President Polk said that he wanted the land between the Río Nueces to the north and the Río Grande to the south, and for Mexico to pay money it owed to certain American citizens. What he really wanted, of course, was what is today New Mexico, Arizona, and California.

Taylor moved south to the Río Grande and Mexican General Mariano Arista attacked, saying that he enjoyed the pleasure of "being the first to start the war."[3]

Polk told Congress, "The cup of forbearance had been exhausted. . . . Mexico has passed the boundary of the United States . . . and shed American blood on American soil."[4] He asked Congress to declare war.

The war was fought almost entirely on Mexican soil. Taylor led an army south onto Mexican territory, and another colorful American leader, General Winfield Scott, planned to attack at Veracruz on the eastern coast.

Scott, six-foot-four and two hundred fifty pounds in a time when six foot was tall, loved pomp and glitter, sporting gold braid and epaulets. His soldiers called him "Old Fuss and Feathers." "Old Rough and Ready" and "Old Fuss and Feathers" were ready to meet an old foe—General Santa Anna.

General Winfield Scott was extremely successful in his battles against Santa Anna. He was an officer for more than fifty years, serving in the War of 1812, the Mexican-American War, and the Civil War.

With ten thousand troops staging an ambitious landing at Veracruz, Scott entered Mexico and headed east toward the capital, Mexico City. He followed much the same route as the original Spanish conqueror Hernando Cortés did in 1519.

Most Americans supported the war, but some did not. John Quincy Adams was against it, as he had been against Texas independence from Mexico. The poet and philosopher Ralph Waldo Emerson warned, "The United States will conquer Mexico, but it will be as the man swallows arsenic which brings him down in turn. Mexico will poison us."[5]

Santa Anna placed part of his twenty-five thousand-person army under the command of General Victoriano Valencia. His orders were reminiscent of the Alamo: "War without pity unto death." When General Valencia failed to halt Scott's westward advance, Santa Anna ordered him shot on sight.

Scott and his army could not be stopped. Winning battle after battle, they moved west and finally conquered Mexico City. They did this even though they were outnumbered, on unfamiliar terrain, and far from home and convenient sources of supply. Some powerful Mexicans even urged Scott to stay on as dictator, hoping that he could be the person who would bring some order and stability to their chaotic nation.

Scott, of course, refused. A treaty was negotiated with Mexico, giving them $15 million (a large sum in 1846) in return for all the Mexican lands as far as the Pacific Coast and north, including California. By June

The chapel of the Alamo as it stands today is a popular tourist attraction in San Antonio, Texas.

1848, the last of the American troops were out of Mexico.

The Lone Star State Today

What had started with Stephen Austin bringing the "Old Three Hundred" families into the northern Mexican state of Texas, had ended with all of Texas and all of present-day New Mexico, Arizona, and California as part of the United States.

Many hundreds of settlers and adventurers had perished in Texas at the hands of the Comanches and Apaches, and from the hardships of an unforgiving land. Americans died at the Alamo, and Mexicans at San Jacinto. In the Mexican-American War, a conflict between two neighbors who today are becoming equals and friendly trading partners, many more died.

Today the Alamo is much different than it was in 1836. Much of it was knocked down by the Mexican Army after the siege to keep it from being used again by the Texans as a fortification.

From 1845 to 1873, its church and old barracks were used as a depot for the quartermaster's department. When the army moved to new quarters, the Catholic Church, who still owned the property, sold it to a private merchant. He used it as a store. In 1880, the state of Texas purchased the church in 1880 and later bought the convento or Long Barrack. Since 1905, the Daughters of the Republic of Texas have been custodians of the site, which is preserved as a shrine to those who gave their lives there in 1836.

Recent archeological activity has helped to learn more about the details of the Alamo's structure, but it is unlikely that a completely clear picture will ever emerge.

In today's Texas, one often sees the ceremonial flying of six flags: Spanish, French, Mexican, Texan, Confederate, and American. The symbolism is clear: Flags change, the land remains.

★ TIMELINE ★

1810—Mexican War for Independence begins.

1821—Mexico secures independence from Spain. Moses Austin is given permission to bring colonists to Texas territory. He dies soon after getting back to Missouri. Stephen Austin leads the settlers to Texas.

1834—Stephen Austin is arrested in Saltillo, Mexico, and thrown in jail.

1834—*April 1*: Santa Anna takes over, repudiates liberalism, and abolishes local government.

1835—*Summer*: Texan colonists clash with Mexican troops at Anahuac. Cos demands the arrest of Travis, and others.

1835—*July 13*: Stephen Austin is released from jail after eighteen months.

1835—*October*: Santa Anna voids the Constitution of 1824 and sets up a powerful central government.

1835—*October 2*: "Come and take it" cannon incident occurs at Gonzales. Open hostilities start.

1835—*October*: The Texan people set up a provisional government.

1835—*October 9*: Cos arrives in San Antonio.

1835—*December 5–10*: Texans attack the Mexican Army led by Cos. The Mexicans surrender.

1836—*January 17*: Houston sends Colonel James Bowie to San Antonio.

1836—*February 23*: Mexican Army arrives at San Antonio and occupies the town. The siege of the Alamo begins.

1836—*February 24*: Travis makes his famous "victory or death" speech.

1836—*March 2*: Texas is declared an independent republic.

1836—*March 6*: Shortly before dawn, the Mexican Army launches an assault against the Alamo. The battle is over by 6:30 A.M.

1836—*March 27*: Following his defeat and surrender at the Battle of the Coleto, Fannin and his command are executed at Goliad.

1836—*April 21*: Houston's army defeats Santa Anna at the Battle of San Jacinto.

1845—*December 29*: Texas is admitted into the United States.

1846—*April 26*: First shots are fired in the Mexican-American War.

1848—*June*: The war ends, and the last American troops leave Mexico.

★ CHAPTER NOTES ★

Chapter 1
1. Bowie to Governor Henry Smith, February 2, 1836, as quoted in Wallace O. Chariton, *100 Days in Texas—The Alamo Letters* (Plano, Tex: Wordware, 1990), p. 204.

Chapter 2
1. Willard H. Rollings, *The Comanche* (New York: Chelsea House Publishers, 1989), p. 37.

2. T.R. Fehrenbach, *Lone Star: A History of Texas and the Texans* (New York: Macmillan, 1968), p. 67.

Chapter 3
1. Albert A. Nofi, *The Alamo and the Texas War for Independence* (Conshohocken, Pa.: Combined Books, 1982), p. 14.

2. Jonathan Kandell, *La Capital: The Biography of Mexico City* (New York: Random House, 1988), p. 296.

3. Ibid., p. 307.

4. Juan Villasenor, *Santa Anna: Napoleon of the West* (St. Louis, Mo.: Copeland Publishing, 1932), p. 96.

5. T.R. Fehrenbach, *Lone Star: A History of Texas and the Texans* (New York: American Legacy Press, 1968), p. 136.

6. Willard Ray, *The Austins—Father and Son* (Seattle, Wash.: Westlake House, 1948), p. 70.

7. Robert Price, *The Annals of Texas History*, vol. 4 (Austin, Tex.: Texas House, 1914), p. 34.

8. Fehrenbach, p. 142.

9. Ibid., p. 143.

Chapter 4
1. T.R. Fehrenbach, *Lone Star: A History of Texas and the Texans* (New York: American Legacy Press, 1968), p. 185.

2. Albert A. Nofi, *The Alamo and the Texas War for Independence* (Conshohocken, Pa.: Combined Books, 1982), p. 36.

3. Robert Price, *The Annals of Texas History*, vol. 4 (Austin, Tex.: Texas House, 1914), p. 189.

4. Fehrenbach, p. 198.

5. Ibid., p. 219.

6. Clifford Hopewell, *James Bowie: The Fighting Man* (Austin, Tex.: Eakin Press, 1994), p. 12.

7. Nofi, p. 160.

8. Ibid., p. 194.

9. Juan Villasenor, *Santa Anna: Napoleon of the West* (St. Louis, Mo.: Copeland Publishing, 1932), p. 141.

Chapter 5

1. Albert A. Nofi, *The Alamo and the Texas War for Independence* (Conshohocken, Pa.: Combined Books, 1982), p. 31.

2. James T. DeShields, *Tall Men With Long Rifles* (San Antonio, Tex: The Naylor Company, 1971), p. 56.

3. Nofi, p. 74.

4. Jeff Long, *Duel of Eagles* (New York: William Morrow & Company, 1990), p. 100.

5. T.R. Fehrenbach, *Lone Star: A History of Texas and the Texans* (New York: American Legacy Press, 1968), p. 210.

6. Archie P. McDonald, *Travis* (Austin, Tex.: Jenkins Publishing Company/The Pemberton Press, 1976), p. 157.

7. DeShields, p. 193.

8. Catherine Reston and Louise Bach, *Tears of the Alamo* (San Marcos, Tex.: San Marcos Publications, 1919), p. 9.

9. Nofi, p. 49.

10. Ibid.

11. Reston and Bach, p. 67.

Chapter 6

1. Clifford Hopewell, *James Bowie: The Fighting Man* (Austin, Tex.: Eakin Press, 1994), p. 117.

2. C. Richard King, *Susanna Dickinson: Messenger of the Alamo* (Austin, Tex.: Shoal Creek Publishers, 1986), p. 35.

3. Archie P. McDonald, *Travis* (Austin, Tex.: Jenkins Publishing Company/The Pemberton Press, 1976), p. 164.

4. Albert A. Nofi, *The Alamo and the Texas War for Independence* (Conshohocken, Pa.: Combined Books, 1982), p. 84.

5. Ibid., p. 108.

6. Ibid., p. 111.

Chapter 7

1. C. Richard King, *Susanna Dickinson: Messenger of the Alamo* (Austin, Tex.: Shoal Creek Publishers, 1986), p. 98.

2. Jesus de la Pena, *Memoirs* (Mexico City: privately published, 1849), p. 68.

3. King, p. 42.

4. de la Pena, p. 81.

Chapter 8

1. Albert A. Nofi, *The Alamo and the Texas War for Independence* (Conshohocken, Pa.: Combined Books, 1982), pp. 130–131.

2. James T. DeShields, *Tall Men With Long Rifles* (San Antonio, Tex: The Naylor Company, 1971), p. 208.

3. C. Richard King, *Susanna Dickinson: Messenger of the Alamo* (Austin, Tex.: Shoal Creek Publishers, 1986), p. 42.

4. Ibid., p. 43.

5. Ibid., p. 49.

6. Nofi, pp. 144–145.

Chapter 9

1. Catherine Reston and Louise Bach, *Tears of the Alamo* (San Marcos, Tex.: San Marcos Publications, 1919), p. 78.

2. Albert A. Nofi, *The Alamo and the Texas War for Independence* (Conshohocken, Pa.: Combined Books, 1982), p. 152.

3. T.R. Fehrenbach, *Lone Star: A History of Texas and the Texans* (New York: American Legacy Press, 1968), p. 232.

4. James T. DeShields, *Tall Men With Long Rifles* (San Antonio, Tex: The Naylor Company, 1971), p. 206.

5. Fehrenbach, p. 234.

6. Juan Villasenor, *Santa Anna: Napoleon of the West* (St. Louis, Mo.: Copeland Publishing, 1932), p. 167.

Chapter 10

1. T.R. Fehrenbach, *Lone Star: A History of Texas and the Texans* (New York: American Legacy Press, 1968), p. 248.

2. Ibid., p. 252.

3. Robert Price, *The Annals of Texas History*, vol. 4 (Austin, Tex.: Texas House, 1914), p. 19.

4. Ibid., p. 42.

5. Ibid., p. 116.

★ FURTHER READING ★

DeShields, James T. *Tall Men with Long Rifles*. San Antonio, Tex.: The Naylor Company, 1971.

Fehrenback, T.R. *Lone Star: A History of Texas and the Texans*. New York: American Legacy Press, 1968.

Hopewell, Clifford. *James Bowie: The Fighting Man*. Austin, Tex.: Eakin Press, 1994.

Kandell, Jonathan. *La Capital: The Biography of Mexico City*. New York: Random House, 1988.

Nofi, Albert A. *The Alamo and the Texas War for Independence*. Conshohocken, Pa.: Combined Books, 1982.

★ INDEX ★

S

San Antonio, 7, 8, 23, 24, 32, 36, 37, 39, 50, 66
San Felipe, 30, 34, 43
San Jacinto, 99, 100, 101, 104, 105, 106, 107, 111, 116
Santa Anna, General Antonio López de, 7, 8, 17, 20, 21, 29, 31, 32, 38, 39, 40, 41, 42, 43, 48, 49, 50, 60, 62, 63, 64–65, 65–66, 67, 68, 69, 70, 71, 73, 74, 75, 76, 77, 80, 81, 84, 85, 88, 89, 90–91, 92, 93, 94, 96, 97, 98, 99, 100, 101, 102, 104, 105–106, 110, 113, 114
Saucedo, Trinidad, 89
Scott, General Winfield, 113, 114
Seeley, Sarah, 30
Seguin, Captain Juan, 68, 92
siege, 51, 57, 59–60, 69, 70, 76, 92, 94, 116
Smith, Erastus "Deaf", 92, 97
Smith, Governor Henry, 8, 30, 34, 110
Spain, 11, 16, 17, 19, 37

T

Taylor, Brigadier General Zachary, 112, 113
Taylor, Edward, 87
Taylor, George, 87
Taylor, James, 87

Tejanos, 62, 88
Tennessee, 32, 33, 34, 87, 88
Texas, 7, 8, 9, 14, 23, 24, 26, 29, 31, 32, 34, 36, 37, 38, 39, 43, 46, 47, 49, 50, 56, 59, 63, 75, 76, 91, 92, 93, 94, 97, 98, 105, 106, 111–112, 116, 117
Texas independence, 8, 57, 85, 86, 106, 114
Texas Revolution, 30, 37, 43, 109
Travis, Lieutenant Colonel William Barret, 8, 31, 43–44, 45, 48,50, 51, 55, 56, 57, 59, 60, 62, 63–64, 65, 68, 70, 73, 75, 76, 77, 78, 79, 80, 82, 87, 88, 100

U

United States, 22, 27, 36, 37, 39, 48, 98, 107, 109, 110, 111, 113, 114, 116
United States Army, 30, 45, 56
United States Congress, 34, 46, 109
Urrea, General José, 95

V

Valencia, General Victoriano, 114
Veracruz, 11, 20, 113, 114
Veramendi, Ursula de, 37